THE
ANTI-
RESUME

THE ANTI-RESUME

A Survival Guide for the First Generation
Graduating Into Uncertainty

KELVIN G. LEE, Ph.D.

THE ANTI-RESUME

Building a Life That Doesn't Fit the Script

A Survival Guide for the First Generation Graduating into Uncertainty

Hardcover ISBN: 9798994231425
Paperback ISBN: 9798994231401
eBook ISBN: 9798994231418

First Edition
Published by Kelvin G. Lee I
Portage, Michigan

Cover design by Kelvin G. Lee I
Interior design by Kelvin G. Lee I

Printed in the United States of America

DEDICATION

To God: *In Whom I live, move, and find my truest self— beyond any title, grade, or achievement.*

To my children: *Mia, Kelvin II, Aniya, Kyra, Kourtney, and Ayden. May you grow into lives that feel like your own.*

To my wife, *Titania, whose unwavering safety and love create the perfect foundation for me to pass on the discipline, independence, and resilience I learned from my mother.*

To my mother, *whose strict love and fierce protection taught me discipline, resilience, and responsibility.*

HOW TO READ THIS BOOK

This book is not meant to be consumed in one sitting.

It's not meant to be read straight through without pause.

It's meant to be lived with.

Some suggestions:

- Read one chapter at a time, then pause

- Do the exercises slowly, over days or weeks

- Skip what doesn't apply to you right now

- Return to chapters multiple times as you grow

- Close the book whenever you need to

- Highlight, underline, dog-ear, argue in the margins

- Share sections with people you trust

You can't do this wrong.

There is no timeline.

There is no test.

This book is here when you need it.

And you are allowed to need it slowly.

TABLE OF CONTENTS

PART I:
PERMISSION AND FOUNDATION

PART II: EXPLORATION

PART III:
INTEGRATION

PART IV:
LIVING IT

I

PERMISSION AND FOUNDATION

1

THE SUCCESS SCRIPT IS BROKEN

The world changed faster than the advice we were given.

I followed the plan.

Maybe you did too.

Study hard.

Get the grades.

Choose the major that sounds responsible.

Work your way toward the kind of job that would make other people nod with approval.

Not because we were naive.

Not because we wanted to be impressive.

But because it was the only path anyone could point to with confidence.

Our parents and teachers weren't wrong.

They were offering the best map they had based on the roads they traveled.

A map that worked in a world where stability was something you could earn through obedience, effort, and patience.

But the world changed faster than the advice did.

And now many of us are living with the quiet confusion that comes when we've done everything "right," only to end up with a life that doesn't feel like ours.

Somewhere along the way, the path from achievement to peace broke.

The formula stopped adding up.

And yet, the pressure remains:

Don't fall behind.

Don't disappoint anyone.

Don't choose wrong.

Don't waste your potential.

Don't make the people who believed in you question if they should have.

It's a heavy thing — trying to build a life while carrying the weight of other people's hopes and expectations.

If no one ever told you this before, let me say it clearly:

You didn't fail the system.

The system stopped fitting the reality.

There is nothing wrong with you for feeling uncertain.

You are not "behind."

You are not lost.

You are simply standing in the space between the old story and a new one that hasn't been written yet.

This book is about learning to write that story.

Not recklessly.

Not rebelliously for its own sake.

Not with slogans or shortcuts.

But slowly, consciously, and with a kind of honesty that takes courage.

This is how you begin to build a life that feels like it belongs to you.

WHY THE OLD STORY DOESN'T FIT ANYMORE

The path we inherited was built for a world that made certain promises:

Work hard → earn stability.

Stay loyal → be rewarded.

Get educated → unlock opportunity.

For a long time, that was true.

Careers moved in straight lines.

Organizations offered training, mentorship, and long-term growth.

You could predict your life with some degree of confidence.

But the ground shifted.

What actually changed:

In 1989, the average college graduate carried $10,000 in student debt (adjusted for inflation: $24,000).

By 2023, that number reached $37,000.

In 1970, housing costs consumed 20% of median income.

By 2023, that rose to 37% in most urban areas.

Between 2000 and 2020, approximately 5 million manufacturing jobs disappeared.

Many were automated.

Others moved overseas.

The promise that education would replace those jobs worked for some.

For others, it created educated unemployment.

Technology changed how value is created.

Global markets reshaped where work happens.

Automation replaced roles before people had time to adjust.

The cost of education grew while the guarantee it once carried faded.

The world did not ask for permission before changing the rules.

And yet, many of us are still living as if the old script is the only responsible option.

There is grief in realizing the story you were handed doesn't work anymore.

Not anger.

Not blame.

Just grief.

Because it means you have to let go of something you were counting on.

But there is also possibility in that realization.

If the old story no longer defines the shape of your life, that means you are free to shape it yourself.

The uncertainty you feel is not evidence of failure.

It is evidence of being alive in a changing world.

And learning to build a life in a changing world requires different skills than the ones we were taught:

- Curiosity instead of certainty

- Experimentation instead of long-term planning

- Internal alignment instead of external approval

- Adaptability instead of linear progression

This is not a crisis of identity.

It is a transition of method.

Your life is not something you choose once.

It's something you learn how to shape over time.

And you are allowed to learn as you go.

This is a good place to pause.

What you just read might have stirred something.

You don't need to process it immediately.

Close the book if you need to.

Come back when you're ready.

CORE EXERCISE:
THE ANTI-EULOGY

Write a short description of the life you do NOT want to wake up inside of 20 years from now.

Consider things like:

- What would leave you feeling empty?

- What kind of work would drain you daily?

- What kind of relationships would feel disconnected or performative?

- What values would you regret betraying?

- What would you regret not trying?

- What would make you feel like a stranger to yourself?

You're not predicting failure.

You're drawing boundaries around your soul.

Example responses from others who've done this:

"I don't want to be someone who stopped making art because it didn't pay enough. I don't want to look back and realize I traded every creative hour for approval I didn't even want."

"I don't want to wake up at 45 and realize I never left my hometown because I was afraid. I don't want safety to have been the only thing I chose."

"I don't want to be the person who worked so hard to make my parents proud that I forgot to figure out what I actually valued."

This is the first act of authorship.

You can put this book down after this chapter and just sit with what you read.

That's enough for today.

2

YOU ARE NOT YOUR PRODUCTIVITY

Your value did not begin with your achievements.

We learn early that our value is something we earn.

Gold stars.

Grades.

Praise.

Scholarships.

Job offers.

Promotions.

Approval comes in exchange for performance, and over time, the two become indistinguishable.

Somewhere along the way, we begin to believe:

"If I stop proving, I stop mattering."

The pressure doesn't always come from what others say directly.

Often, it comes from what we feel responsible for.

For many of us, the people who raised us sacrificed more than they ever spoke aloud.

Their long hours, their quiet endurance, their hope that we might live with a little more ease — these things live inside us.

And with that comes a subtle belief:

"I cannot afford to disappoint them."

So, we work.

We strive.

We push ourselves past tired, past capacity, past joy.

Not because we are chasing achievement for its own sake, but because we are trying to honor the people who believed in us.

But living entirely through responsibility has a cost.

When your worth becomes tied to your output:

- Rest begins to feel like failure

- Slowing down feels like falling behind

- Any moment of uncertainty feels like proof you are not enough

The truth is simpler, and gentler than the story you inherited:

You were a person before you ever produced anything.

Your value did not begin with your achievements.

It will not end if your productivity changes.

You are allowed to be more than what you accomplish.

THE PRODUCTIVITY TRAP: WHAT THE RESEARCH SHOWS

A 2023 study by the American Psychological Association found that 77% of adults aged 23–38 report experiencing symptoms of burnout.

Not laziness.

Burnout.

The same study found that people in this age group work an average of 47 hours per week, with 62% regularly checking work communications outside of work hours.

This is not a personal failure.

This is a design problem.

The tools that were supposed to make work more efficient—email, Slack, Teams, smartphones—instead made us constantly available.

The culture that was supposed to reward hard work increasingly expects endless work.

And many of us absorbed this expectation so deeply that we now enforce it on ourselves, even when no one is watching.

THE FIRST-GENERATION WEIGHT

If you are the first in your family to attend college, or the first to work in a professional setting, or the child of immigrants who rebuilt their lives from scratch, you carry a particular kind of pressure.

Your success is not just yours.

It represents proof that the sacrifice was worth it.

A first-generational professional shared:

"My mom cleaned houses so I could go to college. How do I tell her I'm not sure I want to be a lawyer anymore?"

Another:

"My dad still works night shifts. I can't admit that I'm exhausted working 40 hours a week in an air-conditioned office. I feel ungrateful."

This is real.

The gratitude is real.

The exhaustion is also real.

And both can be true at once.

You can honor the people who raised you AND build a life that feels sustainable to you.

You can be grateful for opportunities AND recognize when those opportunities are costing you your well-being.

Honoring their sacrifice does not mean sacrificing yourself.

If this chapter brought up grief, that's normal.

Grief deserves time, but it is also a gift. It is evident you were connected to something you cared about, hoped for, or loved.

Take a breath before continuing.

REST AS RESISTANCE

The space between doing and being is uncomfortable at first.

When productivity has been your identity, slowing down can feel like disappearing.

But you do not need to disappear.

You only need to return to yourself.

The goal is not to abandon ambition.

Ambition is not the enemy.

Ambition becomes harmful only when it takes the place of identity.

Your work can be meaningful.

Your goals can be real.

But they do not have to determine your worth.

You get to be human here.

Rest is not something you earn.

It is not a reward for productivity.

It is a biological necessity and a human right.

When rest feels rebellious, that's a sign the system has claimed too much of you.

CORE EXERCISE:
THE 168-HOUR AUDIT

This exercise is not about efficiency.

It is about noticing where your life is currently going.

Week 1: Track

For one week, track how you spend your time — gently, without judgment.

Use simple categories:

- Work (paid employment, job searching, career development)

- Care (for yourself, others, your home)

- Connection (time with people who matter)

- Rest (actual rest, not numbing)

- Creation (making, building, expressing)

- Consumption (scrolling, watching, passive intake)

- Transition (commuting, waiting, switching between things)

Week 2: Notice

At the end of the week, look for patterns:

- What gives you energy?

- What drains you?

- What feels meaningful?

- What feels like performance?

- What surprised you?

- What did you not realize was taking up so much space?

Week 3: Adjust

Then ask:

"If I believed my worth was not earned through productivity, how would I want to spend even one of these hours differently?"

Small shifts matter.

One reclaimed hour is the beginning of a different kind of life.

Sample realization from this exercise:

"I realized I was spending 14 hours a week scrolling LinkedIn and job boards, mostly out of anxiety, not strategy. When I re-directed just three of those hours to reaching out to actual people, everything changed. Not because I 'networked better,' but because I felt like a person again instead of a commodity."

Your life is allowed to move at the pace of a person, not a machine.

3

MENTAL HEALTH IN THE AGE OF OPTIMIZATION

You are not struggling because you lack discipline. The world is overwhelming by design.

Many people today believe they should be handling life better than they are.

But this belief comes from misunderstanding the environment we are trying to live inside.

You are not struggling because you lack discipline, resilience, or motivation.

You are struggling because the world you are navigating is overwhelming by design.

NAMING THE PRESSURE

You are expected to:

- Be constantly reachable

- Be constantly improving

- Be constantly informed

- Be constantly relevant

- Be constantly composed

- Be constantly grateful (because others have it worse)

- Be constantly productive (because time is money)

- Be constantly adaptable (because industries change overnight)

Your nervous system was not built for this.

Feeling overwhelmed does not mean you are weak.

It means you are responding normally to a culture of continuous stimulation and evaluation.

THE DATA ON MENTAL HEALTH

Between 2010 and 2023, rates of anxiety and depression among adults aged 18–34 increased by 47%.

This is not a coincidence.

This is not individual weakness.

This is a predictable response to:

- Economic precarity (a significant portion of this generation cannot afford a $400 emergency expense)

- Housing instability (homeownership rates remain considerably low compared to previous generations at the same age)

- Student debt burden that continue to rise substantially over the past two decades

- Climate anxiety (a large majority report worry about environmental collapse)

- Social comparison (constant exposure to curated success via social media)

- Job instability (frequent career changes are becoming more common throughout a lifetime)

You are not fragile.

The conditions are harsh.

OVERWHELM VS. CAPACITY

Overwhelm is not a failure of willpower.

It is a signal that your emotional and physiological capacity is being exceeded.

Think of capacity like a bucket.

Your bucket has a certain size on any given day.

That size changes depending on:

- How much sleep you got

- Whether you feel safe

- Your current stress load

- Whether you're dealing with illness, grief, or transition

- How much emotional support you have

- Whether your basic needs are met

When the demands exceed the size of your bucket, overflow happens.

Overflow looks like:

- Snapping at people you care about

- Losing focus on simple tasks

- Feeling numb or disconnected

- Crying without knowing why

- Lying in bed scrolling instead of doing the thing you need to do

- Avoiding texts, emails, calls

- Feeling like you're watching your life from outside your body

This is not weakness.

This is your system trying to tell you something important:

Slow down. Something needs attention. You need care.

If reading this is activating, prioritize your immediate safety over finishing the chapter.

You can return to this when you're ready.

WHEN TO SEEK PROFESSIONAL SUPPORT

Self-care is necessary.

It is not sufficient for everything.

Consider reaching out to a therapist, counselor, or mental health professional if you notice:

- Persistent feelings of hopelessness lasting more than two weeks

- Thoughts of self-harm or suicide

- Inability to complete basic daily tasks (eating, hygiene, getting out of bed)

- Significant changes in sleep patterns (sleeping too much or too little)

- Using substances to cope

- Withdrawal from all relationships

- Panic attacks that interfere with daily life

This is not failure.

This is recognizing when you need a level of support that friends, family, and self-help cannot provide.

Resources (available 24/7):

- **Crisis Text Line: Text HOME to 741741**

- **National Suicide Prevention Lifeline: 988 (call or text)**

- **NAMI: nami.org (support groups, education, referrals)**

- **Open Path Collective: openpathcollective.org** (affordable therapy, $30–$80/session)

- **Inclusive Therapists: inclusivetherapists.com** (culturally competent therapists)

If cost is a barrier:

- Many therapists offer sliding scale fees—ask

- Graduate training clinics offer low-cost therapy

- Some employers offer Employee Assistance Programs (EAPs) with free sessions

- Telehealth options may be more affordable than in-person

RETURN TO SELF RITUALS

These rituals are not about self-improvement.

They are about remembering that you are a person, not a machine.

These are not tasks.

They are returns.

60-Second Grounding

1. Sit in stillness for one minute

2. Place a hand on your chest

3. Feel your breathing without changing it

4. Notice: "I am here. I am alive. This moment is happening."

Distance Focus

1. Step outside if possible

2. Look at something far away — a tree, a building, the horizon

3. Let your eyes rest from close focus (screens, books, faces)

4. Notice: "There is a world beyond my immediate worry."

Slow Hydration

1. Drink water slowly

2. Feel the temperature, the movement, the pause

3. Notice: "I am caring for my body. This is enough."

Feet on Ground

1. Place both feet flat on the ground

2. Feel the contact. Feel the support.

3. Notice: "I am held by the earth. I do not have to hold everything alone."

The 4–7–8 Breath (for acute anxiety)

1. Inhale through your nose for 4 counts

2. Hold for 7 counts

3. Exhale slowly through your mouth for 8 counts

4. Repeat 3 times

(This activates your parasympathetic nervous system—literally signals to your body that you are safe)

EXERCISE:
YOUR NERVOUS SYSTEM SUPPORT MAP

On a piece of paper, draw three circles labeled: 'Rest', 'Restore', and 'Reconnect'.

Rest = what helps you stop effort.

Examples: Lying down without your phone, taking a nap, saying no to an obligation

Restore = what helps your body settle.

Examples: Taking a shower, gentle stretching, walking slowly, being in nature

Reconnect = what helps you remember you are not alone.

Examples: Texting one safe person, sitting near others, hugging someone you trust

Write one small thing in each circle.

Keep it simple enough to do when you are tired.

Your life does not need optimization.

It needs space to breathe.

And you are allowed to give it that space.

4

WHAT THEY DON'T TELL YOU ABOUT FOLLOWING YOUR PASSION

You don't start life with a passion. You grow one.

We've been told that the key to a meaningful life is to "follow your passion."

It sounds inspiring.

It feels hopeful.

It promises clarity.

But for most people, that phrase does more harm than good.

Because it assumes that your passion is already known, waiting inside you like a seed with a label on it.

It suggests that one day, suddenly, you will just know what you are meant to do.

And if you don't know yet, it can feel like something is wrong with you.

The truth is simpler and more human:

You do not start life with a passion.

You grow one.

WHY THE PASSION MYTH CREATES PRESSURE

If passion is something you're supposed to "find," then every job, class, internship, and opportunity can feel like a test you might fail.

"Was that it?"

"Did I miss it?"

"Why hasn't it shown up for me yet?"

This creates anxiety, urgency, and comparison.

But the people who say "I just knew what I wanted to do" are usually remembering backwards.

They didn't discover passion.

They developed it — over time, through engagement, effort, difficulty, and meaning.

Passion is not a lightning strike.

It is a slow-growing fire.

THE RESEARCH ON PASSION

Stanford psychologist Carol Dweck distinguishes between two passion mindsets:

Fixed Passion Mindset: "My passion is out there waiting to be found. Once I find it, everything will click."

Growth Passion Mindset: "My passion will develop through engagement, learning, and time."

Her research found that people with a growth passion mindset:

- Persist longer through difficulty

- Experience less anxiety about career choices

- Report higher life satisfaction over time

They also found that passions typically take 6–10 years to fully form.

Not six weeks.

Not six months.

Six to ten years.

If you're 24 and don't have a clear passion yet, you're not behind.

You're right on time.

SO HOW DOES PASSION ACTUALLY FORM?

Passion tends to emerge when four things come together:

1. **Curiosity** — Something catches your attention.

Not necessarily dramatically. Just enough to pull you forward.

2. **Time** — You spend enough time with it to get beyond the surface.

Past the beginner awkwardness. Past the first frustrations.

Long enough to build competence.

3. **Skill** — You become competent enough for the activity to feel rewarding.

Competence creates confidence. Confidence creates enjoyment.

Enjoyment deepens engagement.

4. **Impact** — It begins to matter to you or to someone else.

You see how your engagement creates value, solves problems, or serves something larger than yourself.

So instead of asking, "What is my passion?"

A better question is:

"What makes me lean forward?"

What draws your attention without forcing it?

What do you naturally want to understand, improve, explore, or try again?

Passion grows where curiosity is given room to breathe.

YOU CONTAIN MORE THAN ONE POSSIBLE FUTURE

You do not have one "true calling."

You have possibilities.

Think of yourself as a portfolio, not a single identity.

You might be:

- A person who loves helping others solve problems

- A person who comes alive when making things

- A person who learns by exploring new environments

- A person who finds meaning in supporting others

These are not job titles.

They are expressions of self.

Careers change.

Industries shift.

Skillsets evolve.

But the parts of you that feel alive when engaged — those are durable.

Your life will make more sense when you build it from those signals inward.

Examples of portfolio identities:

Karen, 26: "I thought I had to choose between teaching and design. Now I do curriculum design for educational companies. I didn't know this job existed, but it combines the parts of me that feel most alive."

Steven, 28: "I was a mechanical engineer who loved cooking. I spent years thinking I had to pick one. Now I work in food tech, designing kitchen equipment. The path wasn't obvious, but the combination of interests was mine."

Erica, 25: "I'm a writer who loves community organizing. Some months I lean into freelance writing. Other months I lean into grassroots work. My portfolio career looks messy on paper, but it feels whole to me."

CORE EXERCISE:
THE CURIOSITY MAP

This is not about choosing your life path today.

It is about noticing where your attention naturally goes.

Part 1: Gather

On a blank page, write down anything that has recently made you curious:

- A topic you searched online

- A conversation you didn't want to end

- A question you kept thinking about

- A hobby or interest that keeps resurfacing

- Something you find yourself reading about without being assigned

- A problem you notice yourself trying to solve

- An activity where you lose track of time

Don't filter. Don't judge. Just list.

Part 2: Notice energy

Circle the items that make you feel even slightly energized or awake.

Not the things you think you SHOULD be interested in.

The things that actually create a small spark.

Part 3: Explore without commitment

Ask: "What is one small way I could explore this further — without commitment?"

Could you:

- Read one article or book?

- Watch one tutorial?

- Attend one meetup or event?

- Message one person who does this thing?

- Spend one hour trying it yourself?

Remember: You do not need certainty to begin.

You only need a direction worth exploring.

And you are allowed to change direction as you learn.

Passion is not found.

It is formed.

One step at a time.

BREATHE HERE

INTERLUDE
YOU'RE DOING BETTER THAN YOU THINK

You've read four chapters.

Maybe you've done some exercises.

Maybe you haven't.

Both are fine.

If you're reading this book, it means you're already doing the work.

You're questioning.

You're searching.

You're trying to build a life that feels true.

That takes courage.

Most people never pause long enough to ask these questions.

They stay on the treadmill because it feels safer than stepping off.

You stepped off.

You're here.

That matters.

You don't need to have it figured out.

You don't need to complete every exercise.

You don't need to transform overnight.

You're already doing what needs to be done:

You're paying attention.

Take a breath.

You're exactly where you need to be.

II

EXPLORATION

5

THE 90-DAY GENTLE EXPERIMENT

Identity is something you learn from the inside out.

We are often told to make big decisions about our lives.

Choose a major.

Pick a career.

Decide your direction.

The world asks for certainty long before most of us have had enough life to understand what brings us alive.

But identity is not something you choose once.

It is something you learn from the inside out.

This is where gentle experiments come in.

A gentle experiment is a small, low-pressure way to explore something that makes you curious.

Not to commit to it.

Not to prove anything.

Just to see what happens when you place a little bit of your life energy in that direction.

There is no success or failure here.

Only learning.

WHY GENTLE EXPERIMENTS WORK

When you try something in a small way, your attention becomes your teacher.

You begin to notice:

- Where your energy rises

- Where it drains

- What feels natural

- What feels forced

- What draws you back without effort

This is not productivity.

This is listening.

Your life has been giving you signals all along.

A gentle experiment gives you a way to hear them more clearly.

Traditional career advice says: Choose, commit, pursue.

Gentle experimentation says: Try, notice, adjust.

The difference is profound.

One demands certainty before action.

The other allows action to create clarity.

DESIGNING A GENTLE EXPERIMENT

A gentle experiment does not require a plan, a commitment, or a grand declaration.

It only needs to be:

1. **Small** — something you can try without rearranging your life.

Not: "I'm going back to school for graphic design."

Instead: "I'm going to take one online tutorial on Canva this week."

2. **Clear** — you know what you are trying, even if it's tiny.

Not: "I want to explore helping people."

Instead: "I'm going to volunteer for two hours at the community kitchen this Saturday."

3. **Time-bound** — long enough to learn, short enough to release.

Not: "I'm going to become a writer."

Instead: "I'm going to write for 10 minutes every morning for two weeks."

4. Low-stakes — failure costs nothing but a little time.

You're not announcing this to anyone.

You're not investing money.

You're not burning bridges.

You're just... trying.

You are not choosing a future.

You are listening for one.

THE 90-DAY FRAMEWORK

Why 90 days?

• Short enough to feel manageable

• Long enough to get past the novelty phase

- Long enough to build a small amount of competence

- Long enough to notice patterns in your energy and attention

How it works:

Week 1–2: Beginner phase

Everything is new. Everything is awkward. You don't know what you're doing yet.

Your job: Notice what it feels like to be a beginner again.

Week 3–6: Competence building

You start to understand the basics. Small wins appear.

Your job: Notice what skills you're developing. Notice what parts engage you most.

Week 7–10: Pattern recognition

You have enough experience now to see what's working and what's not.

Your job: Notice where your energy goes. What do you look forward to? What do you dread?

Week 11–12: Integration and reflection

You step back and assess the whole arc.

Your job: Ask the two reflection questions (after gentle examples).

REAL EXAMPLES OF GENTLE EXPERIMENTS

Craig, 25, wondered about teaching:

Instead of going back for a teaching credential, Craig volunteered as a tutor one evening a week for 90 days.

Reflection: "I loved the one-on-one connection but realized I hated classroom management. Now I'm exploring instructional design instead—teaching, but through course creation, not classroom presence."

Anita, 27, was curious about therapy/counseling:

Instead of applying to grad school, Anita trained to be a crisis text line volunteer and committed to one 4-hour shift per week for 90 days.

Reflection: "I loved listening and supporting people, but I realized the emotional weight was too much for me to carry as a full-time career. Now I'm looking at HR roles focused on employee well-being—still helping people, but with boundaries."

Karen, 24, kept thinking about sustainable fashion:

Instead of quitting her job, Karen spent 90 days doing two things: following 10 people working in sustainable fashion on social media and thrifting/upcycling one item per week.

Reflection: "I realized I'm more interested in the business/logistics side than the design side. Now I'm looking for roles in supply chain sustainability for fashion companies."

Michael, 26, wanted to work with his hands:

Instead of enrolling in a woodworking program, Michael took a 6-week beginner woodworking class at a community center (one evening per week) and practiced at home on weekends.

Reflection: "I loved it more than I expected. I realized the thing I craved was working with my hands after sitting at a desk all day. Now I'm keeping my day job but building furniture on weekends. It's not my career—it's my sanity."

Notice: None of these experiments "failed."

Each one gave the person information they needed.

REFLECTING ON THE EXPERIMENT

Reflection is where gentle experiments become guidance.

This reflection is not analytical.

It is receptive.

Ask two questions:

1. What did I feel?

(energy, tension, curiosity, boredom, ease, dread, excitement, exhaustion)

Not: "Was I good at it?"

Not: "Could I make money doing this?"

Not: "Would this impress anyone?"

Just: "What did I feel?"

Write it down. Don't judge it. Just notice it.

2. What does that tell me about who I am?

Your feelings are data about your inner landscape.

If you felt energized: What specifically created that energy? The subject matter? The way you were engaging? The people involved? The environment?

If you felt drained: Was it the activity itself, or the conditions surrounding it? (Many people think they hate writing when what they actually hate is writing under pressure or for topics they don't care about.)

This is not about judging how well you did.

It is about noticing what your life is showing you.

Feel → Understand.

Over time, this becomes your internal compass.

WHAT IF THE EXPERIMENT FEELS "MEH"?

That is useful information.

"Meh" often means:

- The timing isn't right

- The format doesn't fit (you might love the subject but hate the delivery method)

- The environment wasn't supportive

- You weren't curious enough yet (it was someone else's suggestion, not yours)

- The experiment was too short to get past the awkward beginner phase

- This direction genuinely isn't for you

All of these are valuable things to learn.

You did not fail.

You learned what doesn't work.

That narrows the field.

That saves you time.

That prevents you from committing to something that would have drained you.

CORE EXERCISE:
DESIGN YOUR FIRST GENTLE EXPERIMENT

Think of something that has been quietly calling to you.

Not loudly. Not urgently.

Just something you've been drawn to in a small way.

Write it down.

Now ask:

"What is the smallest possible way I could explore this in the next week?"

- Keep it small.

- Keep it light.

- Let the experiment teach you, gently.

Brainstorm possibilities:

- Take one class

- Read one book on the topic

- Watch three YouTube tutorials

- Message one person who does this thing and ask them three questions

- Spend one Saturday trying it yourself

- Volunteer for one shift

- Attend one community event related to it

- Shadow someone for a few hours

Choose one.

Write it down.

Put it in your calendar.

Then do it.

Not perfectly.

Just do it.

And afterward, spend 10 minutes writing:

1. What did I feel?

2. What does that tell me about who I am?

Your life will reveal itself one step at a time.

6

FOLLOWING CURIOSITY

Clarity grows out of experience, not before it.

Curiosity rarely arrives as clarity.

It begins as something much quieter:

- A small pull

- A flicker of interest

- A subject you circle back to without intending to

Most of us are taught to choose our direction by thinking our way into certainty.

But clarity is something that grows out of experience, not something we start with.

Curiosity is how your life quietly taps you on the shoulder.

Think of it as breadcrumbs—small signals pointing toward something that matters, even if you're not sure why yet.

Instead of asking, "What should I do with my life?" ask, "What is quietly calling me?"

The difference:

"What should I do with my life?" produces:

- Pressure

- Comparison

- Analysis paralysis

- Fear of choosing wrong

- External validation-seeking

"What is quietly calling me?" produces:

- Curiosity

- Small steps

- Exploration

- Permission to try and adjust

- Internal attention

RECOGNIZING CURIOSITY (VS. EXPECTATION OR OBLIGATION)

Curiosity feels like:

- A question you keep coming back to

- A topic you research without being asked

- A conversation you don't want to end

- An activity where you lose track of time

- A problem you notice yourself trying to solve

- Something you daydream about

- A subject that makes you lean forward

Pressure feels like:

- Something you think you "should" want

- Something that looks good on paper but feels hollow

- Something driven by comparison or fear

- Something that drains you even when you're rested

Obligation feels like:

- Something you're doing for someone else's approval

- Something tied to guilt or duty

- Something you can't imagine saying no to without consequences

- Something that makes you feel trapped

All three can coexist.

You might be curious about law school AND feel pressure about it AND feel obligated to pursue it.

Your job is to learn which voice is which.

ADDITIONAL EXERCISE:
EXPANDED CURIOSITY MAPPING

If you have 5 minutes:

List 3 things that have caught your attention this week.

If you have 30 minutes:

Do the full Curiosity Map from Chapter 4, then identify 2–3 patterns.

If you have time later:

Choose one curiosity and research it for one hour. Notice how you feel during and after.

You don't need certainty to begin exploring.

You only need a direction worth following.

And curiosity is your most reliable compass.

7

IDENTIFYING YOUR VALUES

Your values are not just words. They are how your body responds.

Your values are not just ideals or concepts.

They are the way your body responds when something feels right or wrong, aligned or off, nourishing or draining.

But many of us carry values that aren't actually ours.

We inherited them from family, culture, religion, or the dominant narrative about what makes a good life.

The work is learning to distinguish between:

- Values you were given

- Values you've genuinely chosen

- Values that are emerging as you grow

None of these are wrong.

But you need to know which is which.

THE VALUES SORTING EXERCISE

Below are common values.

Read through them and sort them into three categories:

Category A: This genuinely matters to me. I would feel out of integrity if I violated it.

Category B: Inherited values I am currently questioning, and I'm not sure if it's mine or not.

Category C: Values that belong to the 'Success Script,' not to me.

Common values to sort:

Achievement, Adventure, Authenticity, Autonomy, Balance, Belonging, Compassion, Contribution, Courage, Creativity, Curiosity, Dignity, Ease, Fairness, Family, Financial security, Freedom, Friendship, Generosity, Growth, Health, Honesty, Impact, Independence, Integrity, Joy, Justice, Learning, Legacy, Loyalty, Meaning, Peace, Pleasure, Recognition, Relationships, Rest, Self-expression, Service, Simplicity, Solitude, Spirituality, Stability, Status, Stewardship, Tradition, Trust, Wealth, Wisdom

(Add others that come to mind)

What to do with each category:

Category A: These are your operating values. Use them as your compass. When you feel uncertain, ask: "Which choice honors these values?"

Category B: These need further exploration. Try living according to each one for two weeks and notice how it feels. Does it feel true, or does it feel like performance?

Category C: You're allowed to let these go, even if they're "good" values. Not everything that's good needs to be yours.

REAL EXAMPLES OF INHERITED VS. CHOSEN VALUES

Inherited:

"I was raised to believe that hard work and sacrifice are the highest virtues. But when I actually examined my life, I realized I value rest and creativity more. It felt like betrayal at first. Now it feels like clarity."

Inherited:

"My family values loyalty above all else—you never leave, you never quit, you stay even when it hurts. But I've learned I value integrity more. Sometimes leaving is the most honest thing you can do."

Chosen:

"I thought I was supposed to value status and achievement. But every time I chose those things, I felt hollow. When I finally admitted I value community and creativity more, my whole life made sense."

Chosen:

"My culture values family above individual desires. I still value family deeply, but I've added a value my parents don't have: autonomy. I can honor both. They don't cancel each other out—but I had to make space for my own needs too."

THE THREE QUESTIONS FILTER

When you feel uncertain about a decision, use these questions:

Question 1: Does this move me toward or away from the person I want to become?

Not: "Will this make me successful?"

Not: "Will this impress people?"

Not: "Is this the 'right' choice?"

But: "Does this align with who I'm becoming?"

Question 2: What is the emotional cost of saying yes? What is the emotional cost of saying no?

Every choice has a cost.

The question is not "which choice has no cost?"

The question is "which cost am I willing to pay?"

Examples:

- Saying yes to a prestigious job that requires 60-hour weeks costs you rest, relationships, creativity.

- Saying no costs you the external validation and financial security.

- Which cost feels more aligned with your values?

Neither answer is wrong.

The goal is conscious choice, not perfect choice.

Question 3: If I made this choice and told no one, would I still feel good about it?

This question cuts through the noise of external approval.

If the answer is yes: The choice is probably aligned with your internal compass.

If the answer is no: You might be choosing for optics, approval, or obligation rather than genuine desire.

Neither is always wrong—sometimes we need to make strategic choices for practical reasons.

But you should know which you're doing.

EVERYDAY EXAMPLES

Example 1: A friend asks for your time, but you feel exhausted.

Question 1: Does saying yes move me toward or away from the person I want to become?

"I want to become someone who honors my capacity, not someone who says yes out of guilt."

Question 2: What's the emotional cost of each choice?

"Saying yes costs me rest I desperately need. Saying no costs me feeling like a bad friend. The cost of saying yes is higher right now."

Question 3: If I said no and told no one, would I feel good about it?

"Yes. I would know I made the choice that protected my well-being."

Example 2: You're invited to join something that looks impressive, but it feels heavy.

Question 1: Does this move me toward or away from who I want to become?

"I want to become someone who does meaningful work, not someone who collects impressive titles."

Question 2: What's the emotional cost of each choice?

"Saying yes costs me time, energy, and probably some resentment. Saying no costs me the chance to have this on my resume."

Question 3: If I did it and told no one, would it still feel meaningful?

"No. I realize I'd be doing this for optics, not because I care."

Example 3: You have an hour free.

Question 1: Does this move me toward or away from who I want to become?

"I want to become someone who doesn't numb out with scrolling when I'm tired."

Question 2: What's the emotional cost of each choice?

"Scrolling costs me feeling like I wasted time. Resting intentionally costs me nothing—I just have to give myself permission."

Question 3: If no one knew what I did with this hour, what would feel nourishing?

"Lying on the couch listening to music, Or calling my friend, Or taking a walk."

These small decisions shape your direction more than the big ones.

8

THE SKILLS YOU ALREADY HAVE

Many valuable skills were not learned in a classroom.

If you feel uncertain about what counts as a "real skill," you are not alone.

The world of work has changed faster than the language we use to talk about it.

You already carry valuable skills.

Many were not learned in a classroom—they were shaped through responsibility, community, care, hardship, and showing up.

But those skills often remain invisible because we don't have the vocabulary to name them or the confidence to claim them.

SKILLS GROW IN RELATIONSHIP

Skills grow in relationship:

Something draws your curiosity → you stay with it long enough to understand it → it begins to matter to someone else.

You don't need a degree to have valuable skills.

You need experience, practice, and the ability to articulate what you've learned.

EVERYDAY SELF → PROFESSIONAL SKILL TRANSLATION

What You Do In Life	Professional Skill Name	Where It Applies
Listening with presence	Conflict de-escalation, trust-building, active listening	Counseling, HR, customer service, management (mgmt)
Asking thoughtful questions	Research, interviewing, coaching, needs assessment	Journalism, UX research, consulting, therapy

Staying calm under pressure	Crisis navigation, steady leadership, emotional regulation	Emergency services, healthcare, customer support
Organizing chaos	Workflow planning, project coordination, systems design	Operations, event planning, administration
Caring deeply	Community support, team culture building, emotional intelligence	Social work, education, HR, nonprofit work
Simply explain complex things	Teaching, technical writing, communication design	Training, content creation, education
Noticing what's missing	Problem identification, gap analysis, strategic thinking	Consulting, product mgmt, quality assurance
Making people feel welcome	Hospitality, community building, stakeholder engagement	Events, customer success, team leadership
Managing multiple responsibilities	Prioritization, time management, resource allocation	Project management, operations
Helping people solve problems	Troubleshooting, coaching, customer success	Tech support, consulting, coaching
Translating between groups	Cultural competency, communication, mediation	Diversity work, international business
Learning new things quickly	Adaptability, self-directed learning, agility	Any fast-changing field, startups, technology

HOW TO TRANSLATE YOUR EXPERIENCE

Many people undersell their experience because they don't know how to describe it in terms employers understand.

The translation formula:

What you did + How you did it + What resulted = Professional skill story

Examples:

What you say: "I helped my younger siblings with homework."

What you could say: "Provided educational support and mentorship to family members over 5 years, developing individualized learning approaches based on different learning styles and needs. Built trust through consistent presence and patience."

Skills demonstrated: Tutoring, mentoring, patience, adaptability, relationship-building

What you say: "I organized my friend group's trips."

What you could say: "Coordinated logistics for multi-person events including scheduling, budgeting, venue research, and communication across diverse stakeholders. Managed competing preferences and constraints while staying within budget."

Skills demonstrated: Project management, budget management, stakeholder coordination, problem-solving

What you say: "I worked at my family's restaurant."

What you could say: "Operated in a fast-paced customer service environment requiring quick decision-making, cultural competency, conflict resolution, and multitasking. Managed customer expectations while maintaining quality standards during peak hours."

Skills demonstrated: Customer service, operations, stress management, cultural competency, quality control

What you say: "I've dealt with my own mental health struggles."

What you could say: "Developed deep personal understanding of mental health challenges, treatment systems, and recovery processes. Gained lived experience that informs empathy, crisis recognition, and person-centered support approaches."

Skills demonstrated: Empathy, crisis recognition, mental health literacy, resilience, self-awareness

CORE EXERCISE:
YOUR SKILL RELATIONSHIP MAP

Step 1: Identify moments of contribution

Write down 5–10 moments when you showed up in a way that felt true to you.

These can be:

- Moments when someone needed help and you provided it

- Times when something wasn't working and you figured out how to fix it

- Situations where you stayed calm when others panicked

- Instances when you organized something that felt chaotic

- Conversations where you helped someone feel less alone

- Projects you completed despite obstacles

Step 2: Name what you were doing

For each moment, identify what skills you were using:

- What were you actually doing?

- What made it work?

- What internal resources did you draw on?

Step 3: Notice patterns

Look across your list. Are there skills that show up repeatedly?

These recurring skills are your natural strengths—the things you do well even when no one is watching.

Step 4: Translate into professional language

Take your top 3–5 skills and write them in professional terms using the formula:

What you did + How you did it + What resulted

You already know more than you think.

You can do more than your resume shows.

The work is learning how to name it.

9

BUILDING NEW SKILLS AND COMMUNICATING THEM

You don't always need a formal credential to build a skill.

Worth repeating: You don't always need a formal credential to build a skill.

You need:

- Access to learning resources

- Time to practice

- Feedback on your progress

- A way to apply what you're learning

SKILL-BUILDING PATHWAYS THAT DON'T REQUIRE DEGREES

Online courses (often free or low-cost)

- Coursera, edX, Khan Academy, etc. (free courses from universities)

- YouTube tutorials (for creative, technical, and practical skills)

- Skillshare, Udemy (affordable project-based learning)

- LinkedIn Learning (often free through libraries)

Apprenticeship models

- Volunteering in the field you're curious about

- Internships (including unpaid if financially feasible, or part-time)

- Shadowing professionals for a day

- Informational interviews that turn into mentorship

Project-based learning

- Build something real (a website, a garden, a budget system, a workshop)

- Document your process

- Share your work publicly (blog, portfolio, GitHub, social media)

- Get feedback from people who know the field

Community-based learning

- Join meetups or local groups focused on a skill

- Participate in hackathons, game jams, or creative challenges

- Contribute to open-source projects

- Co-learn with peers (study groups, accountability partners)

Micro-credentials and certificates

- Google Career Certificates (relatively affordable, 3–6 months)

- Professional certifications (project management, HR, data analysis)

- Bootcamps (coding, UX design, data science—expensive but faster than degrees)

WHEN CREDENTIALS ACTUALLY MATTER

Credentials are not always necessary.

But sometimes they are.

Credentials are legally required for:

- Licensed professions (therapy, nursing, law, medicine, teaching in most states, social work, accounting)

- Regulated industries (finance, healthcare, aviation)

- Government positions (many require specific degrees)

Credentials are strongly preferred for:

- Academia and research positions

- Corporate leadership tracks (not always, but often)

- Competitive fields with more applicants than positions

- Industries that haven't caught up to skills-based hiring yet

Credentials matter less for:

- Creative fields (portfolio matters more than degree)

- Tech and startups (skills and projects matter more than credentials)

- Entrepreneurship (no one checks your resume)

- Trades (apprenticeships and certifications matter more than degrees)

- Freelance and contract work (demonstrated ability matters most)

Questions to ask before pursuing a credential:

1. **Is it legally required?** (If yes, you need it. If no, keep asking.)

2. **Is it the only pathway into this field, or are there alternative routes?** (Research people who currently do the job—what are their actual paths?)

3. **What is the ROI (Return on Investment)?** (Cost of credential vs. likely salary increase vs. time invested)

4. **Can I test the field before committing to the credential?** (Gentle experiments before expensive commitments)

5. **Will I be able to afford the credential without taking on debt that limits my freedom?** (If the debt-to-income ratio will trap you, look for alternatives)

COMMUNICATING YOUR SKILLS TO GATEKEEPERS

You have skills.

Now you need to help other people see them.

Resume/CV translation:

Instead of listing job titles and dates, lead with what you actually did and what resulted.

Weak:

"Server at Local Restaurant, 2020–2025"

Stronger:

"Customer Service & Operations, Local Restaurant, 2020–2025"

"Managed high-volume customer interactions in fast-paced environment. Resolved conflicts, coordinated with kitchen staff to ensure quality, trained new employees on service standards. Maintained 95%+ positive customer feedback."

Cover letter translation:

Don't just restate your resume.

Tell the story of your skills in action.

Template:

"When [situation happened], I [action you took] which resulted in [outcome]. This experience taught me [skill], which I would bring to [specific aspect of this role]."

Example:

"When my family's small business struggled during the pandemic, I redesigned our online ordering system, learned basic web development through YouTube tutorials, and coordinated with delivery platforms to expand our reach. Within three months, online orders increased by 40%. This experience taught me how to learn technical skills quickly under pressure and how to solve problems creatively with limited resources—exactly what you're looking for in this operations coordinator role."

Interview translation:

When they ask: "Tell me about a time when..."

Use the STAR method:

- **Situation:** What was the context?

- **Task:** What needed to happen?

- **Action:** What did you specifically do?

- **Result:** What changed because of your action?

Example:

Question: "Tell me about a time you solved a difficult problem."

Weak answer: "I'm a good problem solver. I'm creative and work well under pressure."

Strong answer: "In my last role, our team kept missing deadlines because information was scattered across email, Slack, and shared drives. I researched project management tools, proposed we try Asana, created templates for our workflows, and trained the team over two weeks. Within a month, we cut our project completion time by 30% and reduced miscommunication significantly. That experience showed me how much I enjoy designing systems that help teams work better."

EXERCISE:
SKILL TRANSLATION PRACTICE

Step 1: Choose one experience from your life (job, volunteer work, family responsibility, personal project, challenge you overcame).

Step 2: Write it the way you'd casually describe it to a friend.

Step 3: Translate it using professional language:

- What skills were you using?

- What was the impact?

- How would someone in your target field describe this?

Step 4: Practice saying it out loud until it feels natural, not scripted.

Skills grow from experience.

Credentials signal skills to gatekeepers.

But your ability to articulate your skills determines whether people see them.

BREATHE HERE

INTERLUDE
THIS IS NOT A RACE

You're halfway through the book.

Maybe you've tried some experiments.

Maybe you've reflected on your values.

Maybe you've just been reading.

All of those are enough.

This work doesn't happen on a timeline.

You don't need to:

- Complete all the exercises before moving forward

- Have breakthroughs on schedule

- Transform immediately

- Know your direction yet

Some people read this book in a weekend.

Some people live with it for months.

Both approaches are valid.

The goal is not to finish quickly.

The goal is to stay in conversation with yourself.

And that conversation happens at the pace of a person, not a productivity system.

You're exactly where you need to be.

Keep going.

Or pause.

Both are right.

PAUSE PAGE

Part I gave you permission.

Part II invited you to explore.

Part III will help you integrate.

This is your invitation to pause.

To close the book for a day, a week, however long you need.

To let what you've learned become part of how you think.

When you come back, you'll be ready for the practical work:

understanding money without shame, building real

relationships, navigating transitions with clarity.

That work deserves your full presence.

This book will still be here when you are ready.

P A R T

III

INTEGRATION

UNDERSTANDING YOUR NEEDS (MONEY, PART 1)

Money affects your choices—not your worth.

Money is not your identity.

It affects your life because it affects your choices—not your worth.

This chapter is not about restriction or budgeting.

It is about clarity without judgment.

Most of us were taught that talking about money is impolite, greedy, or uncomfortable.

But not talking about money doesn't make it less important.

It just makes it harder to plan around.

THE MINIMUM VIABLE LIFE

The Minimum Viable Life is not about "surviving on as little as possible."

It is about understanding what you need to feel stable, supported, and like yourself.

Enough is not small.

Enough is steady.

This number is different for everyone because:

- You live in different places (cost of living varies wildly)

- You have different health needs

- You have different responsibilities (caregiving, dependents, debt)

- You have different definitions of what feels sustainable

The goal is to know your number so you can:

- Evaluate job offers clearly

- Make decisions about lifestyle trade-offs

- Reduce financial anxiety

- Understand how much runway you need for transitions or experiments

CORE EXERCISE:
NON-NEGOTIABLES FOR A LIFE THAT FEELS LIKE MINE

Instructions:

- Be honest, not aspirational

- Include everything that supports your actual well-being

- Don't judge your needs

- Approximate is fine—you're seeking clarity, not perfection

Category	Monthly Estimate	Notes on How This Supports Well-Being
Housing (rent/mortgage, utilities, internet, insurance)		Stability, safety, space to rest
Food (groceries, occasional eating out)		Nourishment, energy, connection
Transportation (car, insurance, gas, maintenance, public transit)		Access to work, community, opportunities
Health (insurance, copays, medications, therapy, dental, vision)		Physical and mental wellness
Debt (student loans, credit cards, medical debt)		Financial stability, reduced stress
Savings (emergency fund contribution, future planning)		Security, peace of mind, flexibility
Connection (phone, social activities, gifts)		Relationships, belonging, celebration

Growth (books, courses, workshops, creative supplies)		Learning, development, skill-building
Rest/Joy (hobbies, movement, streaming, things that restore you)		Mental health, pleasure, meaning
Dependents (childcare, pet care, elder care, family support)		Responsibility, love, care for others

Estimated Monthly "Enough" Total: _____

Multiply by 12 for Annual "Enough" Total: _____

SAMPLE "ENOUGH" BUDGETS IN DIFFERENT CONTEXTS

Example 1: Single person, mid-size city, no dependents, no car

Category	Monthly
Rent (shared apartment)	$850
Utilities/Internet	$80
Food	$350
Transportation (bus pass)	$75
Health insurance (marketplace plan)	$200
Therapy (sliding scale)	$120
Student loan payment	$250
Emergency fund contribution	$100
Phone	$50
Social/connection	$100
Rest/hobbies	$75
Total	$2,250/month ($27,000/year)

Example 2: Single person, high cost of living city, with car

Category	Monthly
Rent (studio)	$1,600
Utilities/Internet	$100
Food	$400
Car payment	$300
Car insurance	$150
Gas	$120
Health insurance	$250
Medication	$50
Student loan payment	$400
Savings	$150
Phone	$60
Connection/social	$100
Gym (mental health need)	$80
Total	$3,760/month ($45,120/year)

Example 3: Parent with one child, medium cost of living, shared custody

Category	Monthly
Rent (2-bedroom)	$1,200
Utilities/Internet	$120
Food	$500
Transportation	$100

Health insurance (family plan)	$450
Childcare (part-time)	$600
Student loan	$300
Child expenses	$200
Savings	$100
Phone	$70
Social/connection	$60
Total	$3,700/month ($44,400/year)

What do you notice about your number?

Does it feel:

- Higher than you expected?

- Lower than you feared?

- Clarifying?

- Overwhelming?

All of these responses are valid.

If these numbers feel overwhelming, close the book.

Make tea. Take a walk. Come back tomorrow.

This work will still be here.

If your number feels overwhelming, that's information.

It tells you:

- The gap between your current income and your needs

- Where you might need to problem-solve

- What trade-offs you might need to consider

- What support you might need to seek

The next chapter will explore how to bridge that gap.

CHAPTER

11

BRIDGING THE GAP (MONEY, PART 2)

When income doesn't meet needs, you have options.

If your current income doesn't meet your "enough" number, you have several options.

None of them are perfect.

All of them require trade-offs.

Your job is to choose the trade-offs you can live with.

OPTION 1: REDUCE EXPENSES

Look at your budget and ask:

- What can I reduce without compromising my well-being?

- What can I share with others (housing, transportation, subscriptions)?

- What can I negotiate (rent, bills, debt payments)?

- What can I cut temporarily during a transition period?

Common reductions people make:

- Housing: Roommates, moving to lower-cost area, living with family temporarily

- Food: Cooking more, meal prep, shopping sales, food banks (no shame—they exist for this reason)

- Transportation: Public transit, biking, carpooling, moving closer to work

- Subscriptions: Cutting streaming services, gym memberships (switch to outdoor exercise or YouTube workouts)

- Phone: Switching to budget carriers ($20–40/month instead of $80–100)

Be careful not to cut:

- Healthcare (deferred health problems become expensive emergencies)

- Mental health support (burnout costs more than therapy)

- Food quality (cheap processed food creates health issues later)

- Connection (isolation makes everything harder)

OPTION 2: INCREASE INCOME THROUGH SIDE INCOME

If cutting expenses isn't enough, you need more income.

Side income models (ranked by barrier to entry):

Low barrier:

- Gig work (delivery, rideshare, task-based apps)

- Freelance services in skills you already have (writing, design, tutoring, admin work)

- Selling items you no longer need

- Pet sitting, house sitting, childcare

- Online tutoring or teaching English online

Medium barrier:

- Building a small service business (organizing, cleaning, handyperson work)

- Creating digital products (templates, guides, courses)

- Content creation (YouTube, blog, newsletter—takes time to monetize)

Higher barrier:

- Consulting or coaching (requires established expertise)

- Building a product business (requires capital)

Realistic expectations:

- Side income takes time to build

- Most people start earning $200–500/month in the first few months

- It takes 6–12 months to build to $1,000+/month

- It requires energy you may not have if you're already working full-time

OPTION 3: SEEK SUPPORT AND RESOURCES

There are systems designed to help.

Using them is not failure—it's using tools that exist.

Resources to explore:

- **SNAP (food assistance):** If you qualify, use it. It frees up money for other essentials.

- **Medicaid:** Free or low-cost health insurance for low-income individuals

- **Sliding-scale therapy:** Many therapists offer reduced rates

- **Community resources:** Food banks, free clinics, mutual aid networks

- **Employer benefits:** Check if your employer offers EAP, HSA contributions, commuter benefits, tuition assistance

- **Library resources:** Free books, internet, streaming services, classes, career help

- **Negotiating debt:** Contact student loan servicers about income-driven repayment plans; negotiate medical debt

- **401(k) employer match:** If offered, contribute at least enough to get the full match—it's free money

OPTION 4: MAKE STRATEGIC CAREER MOVES

Sometimes the answer is not side income, but a different primary income source.

Questions to ask:

- Could I earn more in a different role using the same skills?

- Could I negotiate a raise at my current job?

- Could I move to a remote role that allows me to live somewhere cheaper?

- Could I transition to a field with higher earning potential?

- Could I take a short-term higher-paying job to build savings, then transition to meaningful work?

MONEY CHOICES THAT SUPPORT THE ANTI-RESUME LIFE

Money affects your freedom to experiment, take risks, and build a life that feels true.

Here's how to think about money strategically:

Build an emergency fund (even a small one)

Target: 3–6 months of expenses

Reality: Even $1,000 is game-changing

Why it matters:

- Lets you leave toxic situations

- Lets you take risks (gentle experiments, career pivots, saying no to bad opportunities)

- Reduces daily financial anxiety

How to build it:

- Automate even $25/week into a separate savings account

- Save windfalls (tax refunds, gifts, bonuses)

- Use the "pay yourself first" model—save before spending

Reduce high-interest debt first

Not all debt is equal.

High priority to pay off:

- Credit card debt (often 18–25% interest)

- Payday loans (predatory rates)

- Medical debt (negotiate first, pay second)

Lower priority:

- Student loans (often 4–6% interest, income-driven repayment available)

- Car loans (fixed rate, necessary asset)

- Mortgage (if applicable)

Strategy: Pay minimums on everything, put extra money toward highest-interest debt first.

Invest in skills that increase earning potential

If you have any extra money, investing in skill-building can have high ROI:

- $500 for a professional certificate might increase your earning potential by $5,000–10,000/year

- $200 for an online course might open a new career path

- $100/month for language learning might qualify you for international opportunities

High-ROI skill investments:

- Technical skills (coding, data analysis, digital marketing)

- Communication skills (writing, public speaking, presentation)

- Project management certification

- Industry-specific software training (Adobe Creative Suite, Salesforce, Excel advanced skills)

- Language learning for in-demand languages

Geographic arbitrage (if possible)

One of the most powerful financial moves:

- Earn a higher-cost-of-living salary while living in a lower-cost area

- Remote work makes this increasingly possible

Example:

- Earning $60,000 in San Francisco = struggling

- Earning $60,000 remotely while living in a mid-size Midwest city = comfortable

Considerations:

- Not everyone can move (family obligations, immigration status, relationships)

- Quality of life matters beyond cost (community, culture, belonging)

- Some lower-cost areas have fewer job opportunities if remote work doesn't pan out

The "Enough + 20%" Rule

Once you hit your "enough" number, aim for 20% above it.

Why?

- 10% to savings/emergency fund

- 10% to flexibility (trying new things, gentle experiments, rest, unexpected expenses)

This creates breathing room.

You're not in scarcity mode, but you're also not trapped in lifestyle inflation.

WHEN MONEY AND VALUES CONFLICT

Sometimes your values and your financial needs point in different directions.

Common conflicts:

"I want to work in nonprofit/social justice/education, but I need to pay off debt."

"I want to take time to figure out my path, but I can't afford not to work."

"I value rest and balance, but I need to work multiple jobs to survive."

"I want to leave this toxic job, but I can't afford the gap between jobs."

These conflicts are real.

They don't have easy answers.

But they do have conscious answers.

Framework for navigating values/money conflicts:

1. Name the conflict clearly

Write it out: "I value [X] but I need [Y] and they are in tension."

2. Identify the time horizon

Ask: "Is this conflict permanent, or temporary?"

Many people make strategic short-term choices to create long-term freedom:

- Work a higher-paying job you don't love for 2 years to pay off debt, THEN transition to meaningful work

- Live with family temporarily to build savings, THEN move out with a cushion

- Take a stable job while building a side practice, THEN transition when the side income is sufficient

The key word: THEN

You're not abandoning your values.

You're sequencing your life strategically.

3. Calculate the true cost

Every choice has a cost.

- Staying in the high-paying job costs you time, energy, values alignment

- Leaving costs you income, stability, debt payoff speed

Which cost can you live with for now?

4. Build in non-negotiables

Even in survival mode, protect something that matters.

Examples:

- "I'll take this corporate job for now, but I will not sacrifice my therapy appointments."

- "I'll work two jobs for one year, but I will protect Sunday mornings for rest."

- "I'll live with family to save money, but I will maintain one weekly connection point with friends."

Small non-negotiables keep you connected to yourself during strategic compromises.

Example: Real person navigating this conflict

"I graduated with $45,000 in student loans. I wanted to be a teacher, but starting salary in my state is $38,000. I calculated my 'enough' at $40,000 after taxes. Teaching would leave me in survival mode indefinitely.

I decided to work in ed-tech sales for 3 years. Better pay ($65,000), but not my calling. I automated aggressive loan payments ($1,200/month), lived frugally, and saved aggressively.

After 3 years, my loans were paid off and I had $15,000 in savings. Now I'm teaching, earning less, but I can actually afford it. And I don't regret the 3 years—it bought me freedom."

Strategic compromise ≠ selling out.

YOUR MONEY SCRIPT

We all have unconscious beliefs about money that shape our behavior.

These "money scripts" often come from:

- How we saw our parents handle money

- Cultural messages about wealth, poverty, and worth

- Early experiences of scarcity or abundance

- Immigration experience and generational trauma

- Class background and social mobility

Common money scripts:

"**Money is scarce.** There will never be enough."

- Leads to: Hoarding, anxiety, inability to invest in self, decision paralysis

- Alternative script: "Money flows. I can create more. I am resourceful."

"**Wanting money is greedy or shallow.**"

- Leads to: Under-earning, guilt about negotiating, sacrificing financial health for values

- Alternative script: "Money is a tool that supports my values. I can want financial stability and be a good person."

"**I don't deserve financial ease.**"

- Leads to: Self-sabotage, staying in underpaid roles, not negotiating

- Alternative script: "I deserve to have my needs met. Financial stability helps me show up better in the world."

"If I'm not struggling, I'm not working hard enough."

- Leads to: Burnout, rejecting ease, lifestyle inflation to create artificial scarcity

- Alternative script: "Ease is not laziness. I can be productive without suffering."

"My parents sacrificed so much. I must sacrifice too."

- Leads to: Guilt about rest, inability to enjoy success, overwork

Alternative script: "I honor their sacrifice by building a sustainable life, not by suffering."

EXERCISE:
YOUR MONEY SCRIPT EXPLORATION

The stories your parents told you—and the silences they kept

If you have 10 minutes:

Complete these sentences without thinking too hard:

- Money is...

- People who have money are...

- People who don't have money are...

- When I think about my financial future, I feel...

If you have 30 minutes:

Add these:

- The thing I learned about money from my family is...

- If I had enough money, I would...

- I feel guilty about money when...

Then ask:

- Are these beliefs actually true, or are they stories I inherited?

- Do these beliefs serve me, or do they limit me?

- What would I need to believe instead to feel more at peace?

If you have time later:

Choose one limiting belief to rewrite.

Example:

- Old script: "Asking for more money is selfish."

- New script: "Advocating for fair compensation allows me to do my best work."

Write the new script somewhere you'll see it regularly.

Money is one of the most practical barriers to building an anti-resume life.

But it is not an insurmountable one.

With clarity about what you need, creativity about how to get it, and patience with the timeline, you can build both financial stability AND a meaningful life.

They are not mutually exclusive.

They just require strategy, honesty, and time.

12

SEASONS OF TRANSITION

You are not falling behind when you are becoming.

There are seasons in life where the most important changes are not visible from the outside.

These are the seasons where identity is reshaping itself—quietly, slowly, genuinely.

A Becoming Season is a period where the goal is not to prove, achieve, or perform, but to listen, notice, and allow growth to happen from the inside out.

You are not falling behind when you are becoming.

You are becoming someone who can move forward with clarity.

WHY TRANSITION SEASONS MATTER

During transition seasons, you learn:

- What feels meaningful vs. what feels like performance

- What drains you vs. what restores you

- What values are actually yours vs. what you inherited

- What kind of life feels like it belongs to you

You learn yourself—not through pressure, but through presence.

Most people skip this season.

They go from:

- High school → college (no pause)

- College → job (no pause)

- Job → different job (no pause)

- Breakup → new relationship (no pause)

They move so fast they never have time to integrate what they learned or notice who they're becoming.

Transition seasons are not wasted time.

They are the foundation for everything that comes next.

HOW TO RECOGNIZE A BECOMING SEASON

You may be in a Becoming Season if you:

- Feel called to slow down, even if you're "not sure why"

- Question old goals that used to feel certain

- Notice that your old identity no longer fits

- Feel drawn to explore new interests gently

- Need more rest than usual

- Feel like you're "doing nothing" but something internal is shifting

- Experience grief about letting go of old versions of yourself

- Feel simultaneously lost and called toward something unclear

Nothing is wrong.

Something is unfolding.

WHAT A BECOMING SEASON ACTUALLY LOOKS LIKE

It does NOT mean:

- Quitting everything impulsively

- Having no structure or responsibilities

- Sitting around waiting for clarity to arrive

- Avoiding work or contribution

- Isolating completely

It DOES mean:

- Creating space for reflection alongside responsibilities

- Trying small experiments without pressure to commit

- Protecting time for rest and restoration

- Allowing yourself to not have all the answers

- Moving at a pace that feels sustainable

- Checking in with yourself regularly

Real examples of Becoming Seasons:

Example 1: Working a "bridge job" while exploring

"After I left my marketing job, I got a part-time barista position. It paid my bills but didn't drain me. I used my mornings to write, take online classes, and have informational interviews. People asked if I was 'wasting my degree.' But that year taught me what I actually wanted—and I found it."

Example 2: Staying in a stable job while inner work happens

"I didn't quit my job during my Becoming Season. From the outside, nothing changed. But internally, I started therapy, joined a men's group, started journaling. I was doing the identity work that eventually led me to pivot careers a year later. The transition happened inside before it happened outside."

Example 3: Taking a structured gap year

"I graduated and decided to do a service year with AmeriCorps. It paid just enough to live, gave me structure, introduced me to community organizing—and gave me permission to not have my life figured out yet. That year changed everything."

Example 4: Recovering from burnout

"My Becoming Season wasn't a choice—it was forced by a mental health crisis. I had to go on partial leave from work. I spent six months in intensive therapy, rebuilding my relationship with rest. It felt like failure at the time. Now I see it as the year I learned to be human again."

HOW TO HOLD A BECOMING SEASON (PRACTICALLY)

1. Name it

Tell yourself (and select trusted people):

"I'm in a transition season. I'm becoming, not behind."

Naming it reduces shame.

2. Create gentle structure

Even in a Becoming Season, some structure helps:

- Regular sleep/wake times

- A few weekly commitments (part-time work, volunteering, classes)

- One small daily practice (writing, walking, reading)

- Weekly check-ins with yourself

Structure without rigidity.

3. Protect the space

Say no to:

- Opportunities that look good but feel heavy

- Other people's urgency about your timeline

- Pressure to "have it figured out" before you're ready

Say yes to:

- Small experiments

- Conversations with people who get it

- Rest without guilt

- Learning without pressure to perform

4. Track your internal shifts, not external achievements

Instead of "What did I accomplish this week?"

Ask:

- What did I learn about myself?

- What felt aligned?

- What felt forced?

- What patterns am I noticing?

- What's shifting inside me?

5. Find your people

Becoming is harder alone.

Find:

- One person who understands you're in process

- Online communities of people navigating similar transitions

- A therapist or coach if accessible

- Books, podcasts, or writers who validate this season

You don't need a lot of people.

You need the right people.

6. Expect non-linear progress

Some weeks you'll feel clear.

Some weeks you'll feel lost again.

This is normal.

Growth is not linear.

Becoming is not a straight line.

CORE EXERCISE:
NAMING YOUR SEASON

Honoring what served you while acknowledging it no longer fits

Finish the sentence:

"This is my Becoming Season because..."

Examples:

- "...because I need to figure out who I am outside of achievement."

- "...because I'm recovering from burnout and learning what sustainable feels like."

- "...because the path I was on stopped feeling true."

- "...because I'm grieving the loss of my old identity and haven't met the new one yet."

- "...because I graduated and I have no idea what I actually want."

Write without judgment.

Your truth will reveal itself.

WHEN THE BECOMING SEASON ENDS

You'll know a Becoming Season is ending when:

- Clarity begins to emerge (not certainty, but direction)

- Energy returns

- You feel called to build, create, or commit to something

- The grief of letting go transforms into curiosity about what's next

- Small experiments start pointing in a consistent direction

The end of a Becoming Season is not a finish line.

It's the beginning of a new season.

And you'll have other Becoming Seasons in your life.

This is not a one-time event.

It's a recurring season—each time at a deeper level.

Becoming is not a detour.

It is the path.

A LIFE OF MANY PATHS

You are allowed to contain multitudes.

Your life is not meant to fit into a single title or direction.

You are allowed to have many paths over the course of your life, and many identities that come forward at different times.

Most of us were taught to choose one direction and stay with it.

But identity is not fixed.

It evolves.

Your life is a patchwork—every experience, role, challenge, and moment of growth belongs to you.

At the same time, your life also moves in seasons.

Not every identity needs to express at once.

Some parts of you will lead now; others will lead later.

Together, this means you are allowed to live a life of many paths—without being divided, lost, or inconsistent.

YOU CONTAIN MULTITUDES

You are not one thing.

You might be:

- A daughter and a professional

- An artist and an analyst

- A caregiver and a leader

- A student and a teacher

- A creator and a supporter

- A dreamer and a pragmatist

These identities are not in conflict.

They are in conversation.

The goal is not to choose one and abandon the rest.

The goal is to honor which identity needs to lead in this season, while knowing the others are still part of you.

THE PORTFOLIO LIFE

The traditional model: One job. One career. One identity. Linear path.

The emerging model: Multiple income streams. Multiple expressions of self. Non-linear path.

What a portfolio life can look like:

Example 1:

- Part-time nonprofit work (mission-driven)

- Freelance writing (creative outlet)

- Coaching (one-on-one impact)

None of these alone pays all the bills.

Together, they create a life that feels whole.

Example 2:

- Full-time job in tech (financial stability)

- Weekend woodworking (creative expression)

- Volunteer youth mentorship (giving back)

The job pays the bills.

The other two feed the soul.

Example 3:

- Seasonal work (park ranger in summer, ski instructor in winter)

- Remote freelance work (flexible income during transitions)

- Building a small business slowly on the side

Life shaped around seasons, not a single year-round commitment.

Benefits of portfolio life:

- If one part ends, you still have others

- Different parts of you get expressed

- You're less vulnerable to industry changes

- You can experiment without quitting everything

- You build diverse skills

Challenges of portfolio life:

- Requires self-management (no one else structures your time)

- Income can be irregular

- Benefits (health insurance, etc.) are harder to secure

- People will ask "But what do you ACTUALLY do?"

- It can feel scattered until you find the pattern

SEASONS OF IDENTITY

Not every identity needs to express at once.

Some parts of you are active right now.

Other parts are resting.

Active identities:

- Leading your decisions

- Taking up time and energy

- Visible to others

- Currently growing

Resting identities:

- Still part of you, but not leading

- Not gone, just dormant

- Waiting for their season

- Will return when ready

Examples:

"Right now, 'parent' and 'employee' are my active identities. My identity as 'musician' is resting—but it's not gone. When my kids are older, that part of me will come forward again."

"For the past three years, 'student' was my leading identity. Now I'm transitioning to 'professional'—but 'learner' is still there, just in a different form."

"I used to be deeply involved in activism. That was my active identity for years. Right now, I'm in a quieter season—focusing on my own healing. The activist in me isn't dead. She's resting. She'll return when I have capacity again."

CORE EXERCISE:
IDENTITY CONSTELLATION MAP

Step 1: Draw your center

Write your name in the center of a blank page.

Step 2: Draw 5–8 rays outward

These are lines extending from your center, like sun rays.

Step 3: Name your identities

At the end of each line, write a meaningful identity, role, or part of yourself.

These can be:

- Past identities (who you were)

- Present identities (who you are now)

- Emerging identities (who you're becoming)

Examples:

Artist, Daughter, Friend, Teacher, Learner, Caregiver, Writer, Athlete, Activist, Leader, Introvert, Immigrant, Survivor, Builder, Connector, Thinker, Healer

Step 4: Notice they don't cancel each other out

Look at your constellation.

None of these identities make the others less true.

They are all part of who you are becoming.

Step 5: Mark the active ones

Place a small dot or star next to the identities that feel alive right now.

These are the ones in season.

Step 6: Honor the resting ones

The others are not gone—they are simply resting.

They may return.

They may not.

Both are okay.

WHEN IDENTITIES CONFLICT

Sometimes different parts of you want different things.

Common conflicts:

"My professional identity wants stability. My creative identity wants risk."

"My family identity values closeness. My independent identity values space."

"My activist identity believes in radical change. My pragmatist identity believes in incremental steps."

These are not failures.

These are tensions to navigate, not problems to solve.

How to hold conflicting identities:

1. **Name the tension clearly**

"Part of me wants [X]. Another part of me wants [Y]."

2. **Validate both sides**

Both parts have wisdom.

Both parts are trying to protect something important.

3. Ask: "What does each part need?"

Often, you can honor both—not at the same time, but over time.

Example:

"My creative identity needs expression. My pragmatic identity needs financial security. So, I work a stable job four days a week and protect three-day weekends for creative work. It's not perfect, but both parts get fed."

4. Recognize that seasons shift

The identity leading today might not lead tomorrow.

Right now, maybe security leads.

In two years, maybe creativity leads.

You don't have to resolve the tension forever.

You only have to navigate it for now.

EXPLAINING YOUR NON-LINEAR PATH TO OTHERS

People will ask: "So what do you do?"

And if your answer doesn't fit a single box, they'll be confused.

How to answer without apologizing:

Option 1: Lead with your current focus

"Right now, I'm working in [X] while exploring [Y]."

Option 2: Lead with the pattern, not the pieces

"I work at the intersection of [theme 1] and [theme 2]."

Example: "I work at the intersection of education and technology."

(Even if your actual roles are: part-time tutor + freelance UX design)

Option 3: Name your portfolio

"I do a few things: [X], [Y], and [Z]."

Say it confidently.

Don't apologize for not fitting a single box.

Option 4: Redirect to what matters to you

"I'm figuring out how to build a life that lets me [value]. Right now that looks like [current structure]."

What NOT to do:

- Apologize for your path

- Over-explain or justify

- Let their confusion make you feel illegitimate

- Pretend you're more certain than you are

Your non-linear path is not a problem to solve.

It's a life to live.

Your life is not one path.

It is a constellation of identities expressed over time.

Some shine bright now.

Others will shine later.

All of them belong to you.

WHEN IT'S TIME TO PIVOT

Changing direction is not quitting. It is choosing alignment over performance.

When the story you've been telling about your life no longer feels true, it can create a quiet tension inside you.

Not dramatic.

Not urgent.

Just a steady sense of, "This doesn't fit anymore."

A pivot begins long before the first external change.

It begins when your internal narrative shifts.

When who you once were is no longer who you are becoming.

RECOGNIZING A PIVOT MOMENT

Pivots rarely announce themselves clearly.

They begin as whispers:

- The work that once energized you now feels heavy

- You find yourself daydreaming about something different

- You feel successful but hollow

- You're performing a version of yourself that no longer feels true

- You realize you're staying out of obligation, not desire

Signs you might be ready to pivot:

1. **The story you tell about your life stops feeling accurate**

"I used to introduce myself as a lawyer who loved the intellectual challenge. Now when I say it, I feel like I'm reading a script."

2. Your energy patterns shift

"I used to come alive during strategy meetings. Now I feel drained. But when I'm helping my friend with her nonprofit, I have energy for hours."

3. You feel pulled toward something without knowing why

"I keep researching landscape design, even though I'm an accountant. I don't even know why. It just keeps calling me."

4. You start resenting work that used to feel meaningful

"I became a doctor to help people. But the system is so broken that I spend more time on paperwork than patients. I'm starting to resent the thing I once loved."

5. You find yourself saying "I should want this" instead of "I want this"

"I should be grateful for this promotion. I should want the corner office. But I don't. And I feel guilty about that."

These are not signs of instability.

These are signs of growth.

Pivoting takes time.

This chapter isn't asking you to decide today.

GENTLE RELEASE

You do not have to force your life to remain aligned with a past identity.

You are allowed to let go of:

- Roles that have completed their season

- Paths that once fit but no longer do

- Identities you've outgrown

- Dreams that were never really yours

Some things are simply complete now.

You don't have to hold them anymore.

What gentle release looks like:

Not: "I wasted five years in this field. I should have known better."

But: "That path taught me what I needed to learn. Now I'm ready for something different."

Not: "I'm abandoning my degree/training/investment."

But: "I'm building on what I learned, even as I move in a new direction."

Not: "Everyone will think I'm flaky/unstable/lost."

But: "The people who matter will understand that growth sometimes looks like change."

THE GRIEF OF PIVOTING

Pivoting often involves grief.

You're not just leaving a job or changing a path.

You're letting go of:

- The version of yourself who chose this path

- The story you told yourself about who you'd become

- The expectations others had for you

- The investment (time, money, identity) you made

This grief is real.

It deserves space.

You can grieve a path AND still choose to leave it.

You can honor what something gave you AND recognize it's complete.

Both can be true.

What to do with the grief:

- Let yourself feel it (don't rush past it with forced positivity)

- Talk about it with people who understand

- Write about it

- Give yourself a ritual of closure (a letter, a goodbye, a symbolic act)

Grief processed becomes wisdom.

Grief avoided becomes stuck energy.

PIVOTING IS MATURITY, NOT FAILURE

Changing direction is not quitting.

It is choosing alignment over performance.

It is maturity to recognize when a season has ended.

The people who stay in the wrong place out of stubbornness are not more committed.

They are more afraid.

The people who pivot when something stops fitting are not flaky.

They are responsive to their own growth.

Reframing the pivot:

Old story: "I quit. I gave up. I couldn't handle it."

New story: "I completed that chapter. I learned what I needed. Now I'm ready for what's next."

Old story: "I wasted all that time and money."

New story: "Everything I learned is still mine. I'm carrying it into a new context."

Old story: "I'm starting over from scratch."

New story: "I'm beginning again, with more self-knowledge than I had before."

PRACTICAL STEPS FOR PIVOTING

Step 1: Get clear on what's not working

Be specific. Don't just say "I hate my job."

Ask:

- What specifically feels off? (The tasks? The culture? The hours? The values misalignment?)

- What do I dread? What lights me up?

- Is this role the problem, or is this field the problem?

Sometimes you need a different role in the same field.

Sometimes you need a different field entirely.

Step 2: Identify what you want to move toward (not just away from)

It's easier to know what you don't want than what you do want.

But running AWAY from something doesn't give you direction.

Ask:

- What do I want more of in my daily life?

- What kind of work feels meaningful to me now?

- What environment lets me be my best self?

- What values do I need my work to honor?

Step 3: Test the new direction gently before committing

Do NOT:

- Quit your job impulsively

- Enroll in an expensive program before testing the field

- Burn bridges

- Make irreversible decisions in a moment of frustration

DO:

- Try gentle experiments (90 days, remember?)

- Talk to people already doing the work you're considering

- Volunteer, shadow, or freelance in the new field

- Take one class before committing to a degree program

Let your experiments inform your pivot.

Step 4: Build a bridge, not a cliff

Most successful pivots are gradual, not sudden.

Bridge strategies:

- Keep current job while building skills in new field

- Go part-time in current role while testing new direction

- Take a lateral move that gets you closer to where you want to be

- Use savings to fund a transition period (if you have them)

- Find a "bridge job" that pays bills while you explore

Avoid the cliff:

- Quitting with no plan

- Assuming the new field will immediately pay what you need

- Burning through savings without a timeline

- Isolating yourself during the transition

Step 5: Manage the identity shift

Pivoting requires telling a new story about yourself—to yourself and others.

To yourself:

Practice saying:

"I used to be [X]. Now I'm becoming [Y]."

Not: "I used to be [X] but I failed and now I'm lost."

To others:

Practice saying:

"I spent [time period] in [old field], which taught me [skills/insights]. Now I'm applying that experience to [new field]."

Example: "I spent five years in finance, which taught me how to analyze systems and manage complexity. Now I'm applying that to healthcare operations."

You're not starting from zero.

You're building on what you've learned.

Step 6: Find your pivot support system

You need:

- At least one person who believes your pivot makes sense

- People in your target field who can offer guidance

- A therapist/coach if you can access one

- Communities of people who've made similar transitions

You don't need everyone to understand.

You need enough support to keep going.

HANDLING OTHER PEOPLE'S REACTIONS

When you pivot, people will have opinions.

Some will be supportive.

Some will be confused.

Some will project their own fears onto your choice.

Common reactions and how to handle them:

"But you spent so much time/money on [old path]!"

Response: "I did. And I learned a lot. Now I'm ready to apply that learning differently."

(You don't owe them a defense.)

"Aren't you worried about starting over?"

Response: "I'm not starting over. I'm building on what I know."

"What will you do for money?"

Response: "I'm working on a transition plan. I'll figure it out as I go."

(Confidence, not certainty.)

"I could never do that."

Response: "That's okay. We all have different paths."

(Don't argue. Don't explain. They're talking about themselves, not you.)

"What if it doesn't work out?"

Response: "Then I'll adjust. I've adapted before."

For family (especially if they sacrificed for your original path):

This one is harder.

If your family sacrificed for you to become a [doctor/lawyer/engineer/etc.], and now you want to pivot, they may feel hurt, confused, or betrayed.

You can't control their feelings.

But you can communicate with care.

What to say:

"I know you sacrificed a lot to help me get here. I'm so grateful. That path taught me [what it taught you]. But I've learned that [new path] aligns better with who I'm becoming. I'm not abandoning what you gave me—I'm building on it in a different way."

Some will understand immediately.

Some will need time.

Some may never fully understand.

You can honor their sacrifice AND make the choice that's right for you.

Both can be true.

CORE EXERCISE:
WHAT STORY AM I OUTGROWING?

Finish these sentences without overthinking:

1. The story I have been telling about myself is...

Example: "I'm a high achiever who always finishes what she starts."

2. The part of that story that no longer feels true is...

Example: "The part where I have to finish everything I start, even if it's draining me."

3. The person I am becoming now is someone who...

Example: "...honors when something is complete, even if it doesn't look like traditional success."

Let the words come gently.

No urgency.

No pressure.

Your pivot doesn't have to be dramatic.

It just has to be true.

Pivoting is not failure.

It is evolution.

And you are allowed to evolve.

15

RELATIONSHIPS OVER NETWORKING

Connection is built on honesty, not performance.

Networking feels uncomfortable for many people because it teaches us to treat relationships as transactions.

You are encouraged to present a polished version of yourself, to impress, to position, to persuade.

But genuine connection does not begin with performance.

It begins with honesty.

This chapter is about building relationships that actually sustain you—not contacts who might be useful someday, but people who help you stay human.

WHY NETWORKING FEELS WRONG

Networking assumes that the goal of a relationship is an outcome.

You meet someone → you exchange value → you get something you need.

But real relationships are not built on outcomes.

They are built on feeling seen, understood, and supported.

When the purpose of connection is to gain something, trust cannot form.

What networking culture teaches:

- Your value is what you can offer

- Relationships are strategic

- Vulnerability is unprofessional

- Every interaction should advance your career

- If someone can't "help" you, they're not worth your time

What actually builds meaningful relationships:

- Mutual curiosity

- Shared values or experiences

- Genuine care

- Reciprocal support (not transactional—just both people showing up)

- Honesty about where you are

YOUR SUPPORT SYSTEM (NOT YOUR NETWORK)

Your support system is made up of the people who help you stay grounded.

Not the people who are impressed by you, but the people who know you.

Not the people who only show up when things are going well, but the people who stay when life becomes uncertain.

Your support system is not measured in size.

It is measured in depth, in steadiness, in mutual care.

How to recognize supportive people:

1. You feel more like yourself after talking with them

Not performed.

Not impressive.

Just... yourself.

2. You do not feel the need to prove anything

You can be uncertain, messy, in-process, and they don't need you to be more resolved.

3. Your energy feels steadier, not drained

Some people take energy (even when they're "nice").

Some people restore it.

Notice the difference.

4. They listen without trying to fix or evaluate you

They hold space for your experience without needing to solve it or judge it.

5. They remember what matters to you

They ask about the thing you mentioned last time.

They notice when you're off.

They care about the texture of your life, not just the headlines.

These are signs of connection, not networking.

THE SLOW-BONDING MODEL

Meaningful relationships are formed over time, through repeated presence.

Not intensity.

Not admiration.

Not strategy.

Small, consistent interactions over time build trust, understanding, and belonging.

The research on friendship:

It takes approximately:

- 50 hours to move from acquaintance to casual friend

- 90 hours to move from casual friend to friend

- 200+ hours to move to close friend

(Source: Jeffrey Hall, University of Kansas)

You cannot rush depth.

You can only show up consistently and let it build.

What slow bonding looks like:

- Weekly coffee with the same person

- Showing up to the same community event regularly

- Reaching out after difficult conversations, not just fun ones

- Remembering details about their life

- Being present without agenda

This is not efficient.

This is not scalable.

This is how actual relationships form.

BUILDING COMMUNITY IN A FRAGMENTED WORLD

Many people today feel deeply lonely, even when they're constantly "connected."

You can have 500 LinkedIn or Facebook connections and no one to call when you're struggling.

Community is not built through accumulation.

It is built through consistency and vulnerability.

Where to find your people:

1. **Shared practice spaces**

Places where people return regularly to do something together:

- Classes (yoga, dance, art, language, cooking)

- Volunteer organizations

- Community groups (book clubs, hiking groups, maker spaces)

- Faith/spiritual communities

- Activist or mutual aid groups

2. Transition spaces

Places where people are also in-between:

- Career transition groups

- Grief support groups

- New parent groups

- Recovery communities (AA, SMART Recovery, etc.)

- First-gen professional communities

3. Online communities (when chosen carefully)

- Niche Discord or Slack communities around shared interests

- Subreddits or forums focused on specific topics

- Online courses with cohort models

- Patreon or newsletter communities

(Beware: online spaces can also increase loneliness if they're performance-based or comparison-heavy)

4. Work (sometimes)

Not through forced "team building," but through:

- Informal lunch groups

- Shared struggles or projects

- Honest conversations about work-life balance

- Employee resource groups

How to move from "showing up" to "belonging":
Step 1: Show up repeatedly

Go to the same thing more than once.

Familiarity builds safety.

Step 2: Be a little more real each time

Not oversharing immediately.

But slowly letting people see more of who you are.

Step 3: Initiate small connection gestures

- Ask someone to coffee after the group meeting

- Remember something they mentioned and ask about it next time

- Offer help when you notice they need it

- Share something vulnerable and see if they reciprocate

Step 4: Be consistent

Community is built by the people who keep showing up.

WHAT ABOUT PROFESSIONAL CONNECTIONS?

You still need professional connections.

You just don't need to call it "networking."

How to build professional relationships without the ick:

1. Lead with genuine curiosity, not agenda

Don't ask: "Can you help me get a job?"

Do ask: "How did you navigate your transition into this field? What surprised you?"

People can tell when you care about them vs. when you care about what they can do for you.

2. Offer value without expecting immediate return

- Share an article relevant to their work

- Introduce them to someone else they'd benefit from knowing

- Celebrate their wins publicly

- Offer a skill you have that might help them

Generosity builds relationships.

Transactions build contacts.

3. Follow up, but not transactionally

After meeting someone:

- Send a genuine note (not a template)

- Reference something specific from your conversation

- Don't immediately ask for something

Then, periodically:

- Check in when you see their work mentioned somewhere

- Reach out when something reminds you of them

- Engage with their content (if they share publicly)

Stay in loose contact without being strategic about it.

4. Be honest about where you are

Don't pretend to be more established than you are.

It's okay to say:

- "I'm still figuring out my path."

- "I'm exploring a few different directions."

- "I'm in a transition season."

Honesty builds connection faster than polish.

5. Remember: informational interviews are mutual

If you ask for someone's time, bring:

- Specific, thoughtful questions

- Genuine interest in their experience

- Something to offer (even if it's just enthusiastic curiosity)

Don't treat them like a vending machine of advice.

Treat them like a human with a story.

WHAT TO DO WHEN YOU DON'T HAVE COMMUNITY YET

If you're starting from scratch—new city, ended friendships, isolated—building community can feel overwhelming.

Start very small.

Week 1: Find one repeating thing to attend

Could be:

- A weekly class

- A volunteer shift

- A meetup group

- A religious/spiritual service

- A support group

Commit to going at least 4 times before deciding if it's a fit.

Week 2–4: Just show up

Don't pressure yourself to "make friends."

Just be present.

Let people's faces become familiar.

Week 5–8: Make one small gesture

- Introduce yourself to someone

- Ask someone a question after the event

- Compliment someone genuinely

- Sit near the same people each time

Week 9–12: Initiate something small outside the group

- "Want to grab coffee?"

- "I'm going to check out this other event—want to come?"

- "Can I get your number in case I have questions about [topic]?"

Ongoing: Be the consistent one

The person who keeps showing up becomes part of the fabric of the community.

MAINTAINING RELATIONSHIPS ACROSS LIFE TRANSITIONS

When you pivot, transition, or change direction, some relationships will naturally drift.

This is normal.

Not all relationships are meant to last forever.

But some relationships are worth tending, even when life changes.

How to maintain relationships during transitions:

1. Be honest about what you can offer

"I'm in a really intensive season right now. I can't hang out as much, but I still care about you. Can we check in once a month?"

People can work with honesty.

They can't work with disappearing without explanation.

2. Prioritize quality over frequency

You don't need to see people constantly to stay connected.

One meaningful conversation

every few months > weekly surface-level interactions

3. Let people know what you need

"I'm struggling right now. I don't need advice—just someone to listen."

"I'm in a growth season. I need people who can hold space for uncertainty."

Don't expect people to guess.

4. Release relationships that no longer fit without guilt

Some friendships were perfect for a past version of you but don't fit who you're becoming.

You can release them with love.

You can appreciate what they were without forcing them to continue.

Growth sometimes means growing apart.

It's not a failure of the relationship.

It's the natural evolution of life.

CORE EXERCISE:
SUPPORT SYSTEM AUDIT

On a sheet of paper, write down the names of people in your life and sort them into categories:

Category 1: Core Support (1–3 people)

These people help you feel grounded.

You can be real with them.

They stay when things are hard.

Category 2: Nourishing Connection (5–10 people)

You feel energized after time with them.

You don't see them constantly, but the relationship feeds you.

Category 3: Friendly Acquaintances (many)

Pleasant, but not deep.

These are fine to have, but don't mistake them for support.

Category 4: Draining (note without judgment)

You feel worse after interacting with them.

They may be lovely people, but the dynamic doesn't serve you right now.

Then ask:

1. **Do I have at least one person in Category 1?**

(If no, this is your priority to build.)

2. **Am I spending most of my social energy on Categories 3 or 4?**

(If yes, consider redirecting that energy toward building Category 1 or 2 relationships.)

3. **For each person in Category 1 or 2, when did I last reach out?**

(Relationships need tending.)

4. **What is one small way I can show up for one of these relationships this week?**

(Text, call, coffee, letter—something that says "I see you. You matter to me.")

Relationships grow through care, not strategy.

The people who sustain you are not the ones with the best LinkedIn profiles.

They are the ones who know your real name—the one beneath all the titles and credentials.

They are the ones who remind you that you are human, not a brand.

And you find them slowly, by being human first.

BREATHE HERE

INTERLUDE
WHAT MATTERS CANNOT BE MEASURED

You're near the end of the book.

Maybe you've done some exercises.

Maybe you've started some experiments.

Maybe you're still just thinking.

All of those count.

The most important work you're doing might not be visible yet.

You can't measure:

- How you're learning to listen to yourself

- How you're building courage to choose differently

- How you're becoming someone who trusts their own direction

- How you're releasing old stories that never fit

But this work is real.

It's happening.

And it matters more than anything you could put on a resume.

Keep going.

You're building something that can't be quantified.

And that's exactly what makes it worth building.

PART

IV

LIVING IT

16

THE ANTI-RESUME IN PRACTICE

Success is creating a life that feels meaningful to you.

Success is often defined by external measures: title, salary, prestige, appearance.

But these measures do not reflect the inner quality of a life.

They do not measure fulfillment, meaning, or integrity.

Success, in this framework, is not about what you achieve.

It is about creating a life that feels meaningful to you.

WHY THE TRADITIONAL RESUME FALLS SHORT

The resume was never meant to hold a whole life.

It measures what is visible, not what is meaningful.

It tracks:

- Output, not humanity

- Tasks, not wisdom

- Roles, not growth

It cannot show:

- Who you've become through difficulty

- The quiet strengths that carry you

- The care you give that no one sees

- The ways you are reshaping your life from the inside

Most people are not confused because they lack direction.

They are confused because the old definitions of success no longer fit.

This is not a personal failure.

This is a cultural shift.

The work now is different:

- Not to chase certainty, but to learn how to move without needing it

- Not to build a life that looks impressive on paper, but a life that feels true on the inside

THE LIFE DASHBOARD (MEASURING WHAT MATTERS MOST)

These four measures help you evaluate your life from the inside out.

They replace performance metrics with lived experience:

Measure	Guiding Question
Energy Alignment	Does the way I am living give me energy or drain it?
Connection	Do I feel supported and genuinely connected to others?
Self-Respect	Am I living in a way that I can respect myself?
Growth	Am I evolving into someone I am proud to become?

These are not yes/no questions.

They are ongoing check-ins.

How to use the Life Dashboard:

Monthly check-in:

1. Rate each area on a scale of 1–10 (just a gut feeling, not analysis)

2. Notice where you're thriving and where you're struggling

3. Ask: "What one small shift would move me toward more alignment?"

Not: "I need to fix everything immediately."

But: "What's one adjustment I can make this month?"

Example check-in:

Energy Alignment: 4/10

"I'm spending most of my time on things that drain me. I need more creative outlets."

Small shift: "Protect Saturday mornings for writing. No meetings, no obligations."

Connection: 7/10

"I have a few people I can be real with, but I've been isolating lately."

Small shift: "Text one friend this week and actually set a time to connect."

Self-Respect: 6/10

"I keep saying yes to things I don't want to do. I'm avoiding conflict but losing myself."

Small shift: "Practice saying no to one thing this week, even if it's uncomfortable."

Growth: 8/10

"I'm learning a lot. I'm in a becoming season and I can feel myself changing."

Small shift: "Keep journaling. This process is working."

INTEGRATING WORK AND LIFE (NOT BALANCING)

"Work-life balance" assumes work and life are separate, competing forces that need to be kept equal.

But life is not a seesaw.

Work is one expression of who you are, not the definition of your identity.

A fulfilling life integrates work, rest, relationships, and growth.

Integration looks like:

- Work that aligns with your values (even if imperfectly)

- Rest that actually restores you (not just numbing out)

- Relationships that help you stay grounded

- Time for growth and exploration

All four areas matter.

None should consume everything.

Questions to assess integration:

1. Does my work reflect any of my core values?

(If not, can I find ways to bring them in? Or is it time to pivot?)

2. Am I getting rest that actually restores me?

(Or am I just collapsing from exhaustion?)

3. Do I have at least one relationship where I can be fully myself?

(Or am I performing everywhere?)

4. Am I learning and growing, even slowly?

(Or have I stopped evolving?)

CORE EXERCISE:
WRITE YOUR ANTI-RESUME

Instead of listing achievements, degrees, and job titles, the anti-resume lists contribution moments—times when your presence made a meaningful difference, even quietly.

Write down at least five moments using clear, simple language:

- Someone was supported because of you

- Someone felt less alone because you showed up

- Something improved because of your care or consistency

- A situation changed because you stayed grounded

- A person grew because you encouraged them

- You made a choice that honored your integrity, even when it was hard

- You stayed when it would have been easier to leave

- You left when staying would have cost you yourself

- You learned something that changed how you see the world

- You helped someone see themselves more clearly

Examples of anti-resume entries:

"I showed up for my friend every week during her cancer treatment. I didn't have answers. I just sat with her."

"I stayed in a difficult job for two years because my team needed stability during a transition. When I left, three people told me my steadiness helped them survive that period."

"I taught my younger sibling how to stand up for themselves. Now they advocate for others."

"I chose to leave a prestigious position because it required me to compromise my values. It was the hardest and most important decision I've made."

"I built a community garden in my neighborhood. Now 12 families grow food together and actually know each other's names."

"I learned to apologize. I learned to repair harm. I learned that integrity is more important than being right."

"I helped a coworker navigate a mental health crisis. I connected them with resources and checked in for months. They're still here."

These are the moments that matter.

Not because they're impressive.

But because they're true.

These moments will not appear on LinkedIn.

But they are the real proof of a meaningful life.

REDEFINING SUCCESS FOR YOURSELF

Success is not one thing.

It is not the same for everyone.

And it is allowed to change as you change.

Old definition of success:

- High salary

- Impressive title

- External recognition

- Linear upward trajectory

- Never failing

- Always knowing what's next

Possible new definitions of success:

"Success is waking up and feeling like my life belongs to me."

"Success is being able to pay my bills while doing work that doesn't drain my soul."

"Success is having people in my life who know the real me."

"Success is learning to rest without guilt."

"Success is making art, even if no one sees it."

"Success is showing up for my community consistently."

"Success is becoming someone my younger self would be proud of."

"Success is building a life where I don't have to perform."

ADDITIONAL EXERCISE:
YOUR SUCCESS DEFINITION

Complete this sentence:

"Success, for me, means..."

Write without editing.

Let the truth come out.

Don't write what you think you "should" say.

Write what's actually true for you.

Then ask:

"Is my current life moving me toward this definition of success?"

If yes: Keep going. You're on track.

If no: What's one small shift that would bring you closer?

LIVING THE ANTI-RESUME DAILY

The anti-resume is not just a reflection exercise.

It's a way of living.

Daily practices of anti-resume living:

1. **Lead with values, not optics**

Before making a decision, ask:

"Does this align with who I want to become?"

Not: "Will this look good?"

2. **Measure progress by internal shifts, not external achievements**

Instead of: "What did I accomplish today?"

Ask: "What did I learn about myself today?"

3. Celebrate contribution moments

Keep a journal or note on your phone where you record:

- Moments when you showed up for someone

- Moments when you acted with integrity

- Moments when you grew

These moments are evidence of a life well-lived.

4. Check in with your Life Dashboard monthly

Energy, Connection, Self-Respect, Growth.

Are you tending all four?

5. Surround yourself with people who see the real you

Not people who are impressed by your resume.

People who know your heart.

Your life is not a performance.

It is not a brand.

It is not a competition.

It is yours.

And the anti-resume is how you remember that.

17

LEARNING TO ADAPT

The only future-proof skill is responsiveness.

Most of us were taught to make decisions as if the world would stay still.

But the world is not still.

It shifts, evolves, and reshapes itself faster than any of us can predict.

We are not meant to build a fixed identity in a moving world.

We are meant to grow with the world as it changes.

YOU DON'T NEED A FINAL IDENTITY

You are allowed to change your mind, your direction, your pace, and your priorities.

Identity is not a contract—it is a conversation with your life.

Your future self is not someone you need to predict.

They are someone you will meet.

And you will meet them by staying responsive to what's happening now, not by planning every detail in advance.

THE ONLY FUTURE-PROOF SKILL: ADAPTATION

Adaptation is not about being prepared for everything.

It is about staying responsive to what is happening now.

Adaptation sounds like:

- I can adjust.

- I can learn as I go.

- I do not need to have the entire path to take one next step.

- I can begin again without shame.

- My direction can change as I change.

What helps you adapt:

- Regular check-ins with yourself (weekly, monthly, quarterly)

- Gentle experiments that test new directions before committing

- A support system that knows you're in process

- Self-compassion when things don't go as planned

- Curiosity about change rather than fear of it

LEARNING AS A LIFE PRACTICE

Learning is not something that ends when you choose a job, a path, or a direction.

It continues quietly, through curiosity, reflection, and presence.

You do not have to master your life.

You only have to stay in relationship with it.

The people who navigate uncertainty best are not the ones with the most certainty.

They are the ones who have learned to stay in dialogue with their own experience.

They ask themselves regularly:

- What is my life showing me right now?

- What feels aligned?

- What feels off?

- What needs to shift?

- What do I need to learn?

- Where do I need support?

And they adjust accordingly.

CORE EXERCISE:
YOUR LEARNING OPERATING SYSTEM

Instead of asking "What should I do with my life?" try asking these three questions regularly (weekly or monthly):

1. What is my life showing me right now?

Look for patterns:

- What keeps coming up?

- What feels easier than it used to?

- What feels harder?

- What am I drawn toward?

- What am I avoiding?

- Where is my energy going?

- What feedback am I receiving from the world?

2. What feels gentle and possible as a next step?

Not: "What's the five-year plan?"

But: "What's one small move I could make this week that feels aligned?"

3. How can I adjust without forcing or rushing?

Not: "I need to figure this out RIGHT NOW."

But: "What's one small shift I can make that honors where I am?"

Write your answers somewhere you can return to.

Let them change as you do.

This is not a one-time exercise.

This is a practice of staying in conversation with yourself.

There is no final version of you.

Your life does not need to resolve for it to be meaningful.

You are allowed to continue becoming.

CONCLUSION
PERMISSION TO BE UNCERTAIN

You don't have to have everything figured out to be living a real life.

You don't have to move faster than your capacity.

You don't have to prove anything to be worthy of being here.

Your life is not late.

You are not behind.

I don't know what your path will look like from here.

And I don't need to.

Because the point was never to choose the perfect direction.

The point is that you are allowed to listen to your life.

You are allowed to learn your way forward.

You are allowed to change your mind, to pause, to rest, to begin again gently.

You are building a life that feels like it belongs to you.

Not a performance.

Not a resume.

Not an identity that needs defending.

Just a life.

Honest.

Living.

Yours.

As you go, remember this:

- You are allowed to take your time.

- You are allowed to move at the pace of your own becoming.

- You are allowed to not know the ending.

- You are allowed to have multiple paths over the course of your life.

- You are allowed to rest without earning it.

- You are allowed to pivot when something stops fitting.

- You are allowed to value things that don't show up on a resume.

- You are allowed to build a life that looks different from what you imagined.

You have space.

You have time.

You have room to grow.

And you don't have to do any of it alone.

Take a breath.

Take one step, when you're ready.

I'm right here with you.

WHERE TO GO FROM HERE

Start small. There is no rush.

These are gentle next steps—not goals, not tasks, not expectations.

1. **Notice your energy**

Once a day, ask: "Does this give me life or drain me?"

Let that answer matter.

2. **Choose one tiny experiment**

Not a plan. Not a commitment.

Just one small curiosity to explore for a week.

(Go back to Chapter 5 if you need help designing it.)

3. Reach out to one person who helps you feel grounded

Not to network. Not to impress.

Just to be real.

4. Write one entry in your anti-resume

One moment when you showed up.

One moment that mattered.

Let yourself see your own quiet strength.

5. Give yourself permission

Write this somewhere you'll see it:

"I am allowed to take my time.

I am allowed to move at the pace of my own becoming.

I am allowed to not know the ending."

You don't have to transform your life all at once.

You just have to stay in conversation with it.

One gentle step at a time.

This is not a roadmap.

It is a toolkit for listening to your life.

Use what serves you.

Leave what doesn't.

And remember:

You are simply living in a world where the old answers stopped working.

And there is nothing wrong with your uncertainty.

You are not behind.

Your life is not late.

You are exactly where you need to be to take the next step.

APPENDIX

ADDITIONAL RESOURCES

Books That Might Resonate:

- *Designing Your Life* by Bill Burnett and Dave Evans (for more structured exercises)

- *The Crossroads of Should and Must* by Elle Luna (on following authentic direction)

- *Laziness Does Not Exist* by Devon Price (on unlearning productivity culture)

- *How to Do Nothing* by Jenny Odell (on resisting attention economy)

- *The Body Keeps the Score* by Bessel van der Kolk (on trauma and healing)

- *Maybe You Should Talk to Someone* by Lori Gottlieb (on therapy and growth)

Online Communities:

- r/careerguidance, r/findapath (Reddit)

- The Creative Independent (creative career advice)

- 80,000 Hours (career planning for impact)

Mental Health Resources (Available 24/7):

- Crisis Text Line: Text HOME to 741741

- National Suicide Prevention Lifeline: 988

- NAMI: nami.org

- Open Path Collective: openpathcollective.org

- Inclusive Therapists: inclusivetherapists.com

Financial Literacy:

- Your Money or Your Life by Vicki Robin

- r/personalfinance wiki (comprehensive free resource)

- Mr. Money Mustache (financial independence)

First-Gen and Immigrant Resources:

• First-Generation Professionals (online community)

• I'm First (imfirst.org)

• My Undocumented Life (resources for undocumented folks)

REFERENCES

RESEARCH AND STUDIES CITED

American Psychological Association. (2023). Stress in America 2023: A national mental health crisis. APA. http://www.apa.org/news/press/releases/stress

Dweck, C. S. (2006). *Mindset: The new psychology of success.* Random House.

Hall, J. A. (2019). How many hours does it take to make a friend? Journal of Social and Personal Relationships, 36(4), 1278–1296. https://doi.org/10.1177/0265407518761225

Pew Research Center. (2020). *Economic mobility and the American Dream.* https://www.pewresearch.org/social-trends/

U.S. Bureau of Labor Statistics. (2022). *Number of jobs, labor market experience, and earnings growth among Americans at 55.* https://www.bls.gov/

Vallerand, R. J., et al. (2003). Les passions de l'âme: On obsessive and harmonious passion. *Journal of Personality and Social Psychology, 85*(4), 756–767.

BOOKS FOR FURTHER READING

Burnett, B., & Evans, D. (2016*). Designing your life: How to build a well-lived, joyful life.* Alfred A. Knopf.

Luna, E. (2015). *The crossroads of should and must: Find and follow your passion.* Workman Publishing.

Odell, J. (2019). *How to do nothing: Resisting the attention economy.* Melville House.

Price, D. (2021). *Laziness does not exist.* Atria Books.

Robin, V., & Dominguez, J. (2018). *Your money or your life: 9 steps to transforming your relationship with money and achieving financial independence.* Penguin Books.

van der Kolk, B. (2014). *The body keeps the score: Brain, mind, and body in the healing of trauma.* Penguin Books.

MENTAL HEALTH RESOURCES

Crisis Text Line. Text HOME to 741741. Available 24/7.
https://www.crisistextline.org/

Inclusive Therapists. Directory of culturally competent mental
health professionals.
https://www.inclusivetherapists.com/

National Alliance on Mental Illness (NAMI). Support groups,
education, and referrals.
https://www.nami.org/

National Suicide Prevention Lifeline. Call or text 988. Available
24/7.
https://988lifeline.org/

Open Path Collective. Affordable therapy ($30–$80/session).
https://openpathcollective.org/

FINANCIAL RESOURCES

Mr. Money Mustache. Financial independence and intentional
living.
https://www.mrmoneymustache.com/

Personal Finance Wiki (Reddit). Comprehensive free financial
education.
https://www.reddit.com/r/personalfinance/wiki/

U.S. Department of Agriculture SNAP. Food assistance program
information.
https://www.fns.usda.gov/snap

FIRST-GENERATION AND IMMIGRANT RESOURCES

First-Generation Professionals. Online community and resources.
https://www.firstgenprofessionals.org/

I'm First. Support for first-generation college students.
https://imfirst.org/

My Undocumented Life. Resources for undocumented
individuals.
https://mydocumentedlife.org/

CAREER AND COMMUNITY RESOURCES

80,000 Hours. Career planning for social impact.
https://80000hours.org/

The Creative Independent. Advice for creative people.
https://thecreativeindependent.com/

r/careerguidance, r/findapath. Reddit communities for career
exploration.
https://www.reddit.com/

ONLINE LEARNING PLATFORMS

Coursera. Free and paid courses from universities.
    https://www.coursera.org/

edX. Free online courses.
    https://www.edx.org/

Khan Academy. Free educational resources.
    https://www.khanacademy.org/

LinkedIn Learning. Professional development courses (often
    free through libraries).
    https://www.linkedin.com/learning/

Skillshare. Creative and practical skills courses.
    https://www.skillshare.com/

Udemy. Affordable online courses.
    https://www.udemy.com/

YouTube. Free tutorials on virtually any skill.
    https://www.youtube.com/

NOTE ON SOURCES

This book draws on personal interviews, reader submissions, and professional experience in addition to published research. All individual stories and examples have been shared with permission and, where requested, identifying details have been changed to protect privacy. Statistical data and research findings are cited from publicly available sources current as of 2025.

ABOUT THE AUTHOR

Kelvin G. Lee, Ph.D., spent thirty years following the scripts of leadership and academia before realizing the most important story he had to write was his own. A Navy veteran, educator, and organizational leader, he now focuses on helping others find the courage to build lives that feel true rather than just impressive.